"If you are looking for a daily tool to help you understand the overall story of Scripture while also challenging you to grow spiritually, then *Exodus: Stories of Redemption and Relationship* is exactly what you need. David Murray has eloquently crafted daily studies that are as deep as they are accessible. In fifty days of study, David walks you through one of the most well-known stories in the Bible in a fresh way that will make you grapple with your own need for God and his redeeming work."

**Adam Griffin,** Lead Pastor, Eastside Community Church, Dallas, Texas; Host, *Family Discipleship Podcast*; coauthor, *Family Discipleship*

"Exodus is foundational for the story of the Bible and the story of God's work among his people, and this book is a wonderful companion in your journey through Exodus. In it, David Murray helps us to see clearly how Exodus not only fits into the story of the Bible that culminates in Christ but also how the story continues in us, his church. I am happy to recommend this devotional as a complement to your own reading through Exodus so that you are better equipped both to change your own story with God's story and help others do the same."

**Chris Bruno,** Global Partner for Hawaii and the Pacific Islands, Training Leaders International; author, *The Whole Story of the Bible in 16 Verses*

"If you are looking for a biblically based devotional book that is surprisingly accessible to any level of Christian maturity, you have picked up the right book. This particular book on Exodus is uniquely useful because David Murray wrote it. He has a special writing gift that demonstrates his skill as an expositor and his shepherding intuition as a pastor. That gift is wonderfully present in this particular volume on Exodus, and I commend this book to pastors to buy in bulk and distribute to your entire congregation to study together."

**Brian Croft,** Executive Director, Practical Shepherding

"We live in a confusing swirl of stories—our own and those presented to us by the world. David Murray has crafted something exceptional in the StoryChanger *Exodus* devotional—brief, energetic, accessible devotions on a critically important Bible book that will help us understand God's story and, in the process, find transformation for our own!"

**Peter Mead,** Pastor, Trinity Chippenham; Founder, BiblicalPreaching.net

# Exodus

**The StoryChanger Devotional Series**

By David Murray

*Exodus: Stories of Redemption and Relationship*

*Luke: Stories of Mission and Mercy*

# Exodus

Stories of Redemption and Relationship

David Murray

WHEATON, ILLINOIS

*Exodus: Stories of Redemption and Relationship*



Published by Crossway
1300 Crescent Street
Wheaton, Illinois 60187



Published in association with the literary agency of Legacy, LLC, 501 N. Orlando Avenue, Suite #313-348, Winter Park, FL 32789

Cover image and design: Jordan Singer

First printing 2022

Printed in the United States of America



All emphases in Scripture quotations have been added by the author.

Trade paperback ISBN: 978-1-4335-8093-2
ePub ISBN: 978-1-4335- 8096-3
PDF ISBN: 978-1-4335- 8094-9
Mobipocket ISBN: 978-1-4335-8095-6

**Library of Congress Cataloging-in-Publication Data**

Names: Murray, David, 1966 May 28– author.
Title: Exodus : stories of redemption and relationship / David Murray.
Description: Wheaton, Illinois : Crossway, [2023] | Series: The storychanger devotional | Includes bibliographical references.
Identifiers: LCCN 2022011812 (print) | LCCN 2022011813 (ebook) | ISBN 9781433580932 (trade paperback) | ISBN 9781433580949 (pdf) | ISBN 9781433580956 (mobipocket) | ISBN 9781433580963 (epub)
Subjects: LCSH: Bible. Exodus—Devotional use. | Bible. Exodus—Commentaries.
Classification: LCC BS1245.54 .M87 2023 (print) | LCC BS1245.54 (ebook) | DDC 222/.12—dc23/eng/20220615
LC record available at https://lccn.loc.gov/2022011812
LC ebook record available at https://lccn.loc.gov/2022011813

Crossway is a publishing ministry of Good News Publishers.

VP 32 31 30 29 28 27 26 25 24 23
15 14 13 12 11 10 9 8 7 6 5 4 3 2 1

*Dedicated to my twin brother, Kenny, who has taught me so much about redemptive relationships.*

# Contents

Introduction to the StoryChanger Devotionals 13

Introduction to *Exodus: Stories of Redemption and Relationship* 17

1 God's Unbreakable Promise to the Broken (Exodus 1:1–22) 19

2 Faith Makes the Impossible Possible (Exodus 2:1–10) 23

3 Change Your Glasses to Change Your Choices (Exodus 2:11–15) 27

4 God Comes Down to Lift You Up (Exodus 3:1–12) 31

5 What a Powerful Name It Is! (Exodus 3:13–22) 35

6 God's Compassion for Doubters (Exodus 4:1–17) 39

7 His Rage We Can Endure, for Lo, His Doom Is Sure (Exodus 5) 43

8 A Concrete Covenant for Sandy Faith (Exodus 6:1–13) 47

9 Hardness Makes It Harder (Exodus 7) 51

10 Are Plagues and Pandemics the Finger of God? (Exodus 8) 55

11 God's Purpose for the Wicked (Exodus 9) 59

12 Faker, Fighter, or Faith (Exodus 10) *63*

13 God's Everywhere Goodness Serves Particular Grace (Exodus 11) *67*

14 An Antidote for Amnesia (Exodus 12:1–14) *71*

15 God's Hand and Our Hands (Exodus 13:1–10) *75*

16 Extreme Salvation for Extreme Sinners (Exodus 13:11–16) *79*

17 God's Surprising Solution to Our Greatest Problem (Exodus 14) *83*

18 What Songs Should We Sing? (Exodus 15:1–21) *87*

19 The God Who Heals (Exodus 15:22–27) *91*

20 Complainers or Praisers? (Exodus 16:1–12) *95*

21 The Secret to Exam Success (Exodus 16:13–36) *99*

22 God Takes an Exam (Exodus 17:1–7) *103*

23 Faith and Family (Exodus 18:1–12) *107*

24 The Blessing of Law and Order (Exodus 18:13–27) *111*

25 The Four *R*'s (Exodus 19:1–6) *115*

26 The Love of God in the Law of God (Exodus 20) *119*

27 The Defender of the Defenseless (Exodus 21:1–11) *123*

28 An Eye for an Eye (Exodus 21:12–36) *127*

29 How to Become Debt Free (Exodus 22:1–15) *131*

30 Take the Year Off! (Exodus 23:10–13) *135*

31 God Goes before You (Exodus 23:20–33) *139*

32 God Enjoys You (Exodus 24) *143*

33 God's Living Room (Exodus 25:1–9) *147*

34 God's Favorite Chair (Exodus 25:10–22) *151*

35 God's Supper Table (Exodus 25:23–30) *155*

36 God's Lamp (Exodus 25:31–40) *159*

37 God's Curtains (Exodus 26) *163*

38 God's Fireplace (Exodus 27:1–8) *167*

39 What a Friend We Have in Jesus (Exodus 28–29) *171*

40 The Perfume of Prayer (Exodus 30:1–10, 22–38) *175*

41 I Won't Forget the Man Who Died (Exodus 30:11–16) *179*

42 God's Washroom (Exodus 30:17–21) *183*

43 The Beauty and Dignity of Manual Labor (Exodus 31:1–11) *187*

44 God Works for Our Rest (Exodus 31:12–18) *191*

45 A Persuasive Prayer for the Backslidden (Exodus 32:1–14) *195*

46 Punishing Sin and Praying for Sinners (Exodus 32:15–35) *199*

47 God's Absence Is Our Terror (Exodus 33:1–17) *203*

48 God's Goodness Is His Glory (Exodus 33:18–34:7) *207*

49 Freely Gotten, Freely Giving (Exodus 35–36) *211*

50 The Ever-Living, Never-Leaving God (Exodus 40:33–38) *215*

# Introduction to the StoryChanger Devotionals

Do you want to know the Bible's Story better, but don't know how? Do you want to change your story, but don't know how? Do you want to share the Bible's Story and the way it has changed your story, but don't know how? The StoryChanger Devotional series is the answer to this triple *how*.

*How can I know the Bible better?* At different points in my Christian life, I've tried to use various helps to go deeper in personal Bible study, but I found commentaries were too long and technical, whereas study Bibles were too brief and not practical.

*How can I change my life for the better?* I knew the Bible's Story was meant to change my story but couldn't figure out how to connect God's Story with my story in a transformative way. I was stuck, static, and frustrated at my lack of change, growth, and progress.

*How can I share God's Story better?* I've often been embarrassed by how slow and ineffective I am at sharing God's Story one-on-one. I know God's Story relates to other people's stories and that God's Story can change others' stories for the better, but I'm reluctant to seek out opportunities and hesitant when they arise.

So how about a series of books that teach us the Bible's Story in a way that helps to change our story and equips us to tell the Story to others? Or, to put it another way, how about books that teach us God's Story in a way that changes ours and others' stories?

After writing *The StoryChanger: How God Rewrites Our Story by Inviting Us into His* as an introduction to Jesus as the transformer of our stories, I thought, "Okay, what now? That's the theory, what about the practice? That's the introduction, but what about the next chapters? Jesus is the StoryChanger, but how can his Story change my story in practical ways on a daily basis? And how do I share his life-changing Story with others?"

I looked for daily devotionals that would take me through books of the Bible in a way that explained God's Story, changed my story, and equipped me to tell God's Story to others in a life-changing way. When I couldn't find any resources that had all three elements, I thought, "I'll write some devotionals for myself to help me know God's Story, change my story, and tell the story to others."

A few weeks later COVID hit, and I decided to start sharing these devotionals with the congregation I was serving at the time. I wanted to keep them connected with God and one another through that painful period of prolonged isolation from church and from one another.

I found that, like myself, people seemed to be hungry for daily devotionals that were more than emotional. They enjoyed daily devotionals that were educational, transformational, and missional. We worked our way verse-by-verse through books of the Bible with a focus on brevity, simplicity, clarity, practicality, and shareability. The StoryChanger started changing our stories with his Story, turning us into storytellers and therefore storychangers too.

Although these devotionals will take only about five minutes a day, I'm not promising you quick fixes. No, the StoryChanger usually changes our stories little by little. But over months and years of exposure to the StoryChanger's Story, he rewrites our story, and, through us, rewrites others' stories too.

To encourage you, I invite you to join the StoryChangers community at www.thestorychanger.life. There you can sign up for the weekly StoryChangers newsletter and subscribe to the StoryChangers podcast. Let's build a community of storychangers, committed Christians who dedicate themselves to knowing God's Story better, being changed by God's Story for the better, and sharing God's Story better. We'll meet the StoryChanger, have our stories changed, and become storychangers. I look forward to meeting you there and together changing stories with God's Story.[1]

1 Some of this content originally appeared on *The Living the Bible* podcast, which has since been replaced by *The StoryChanger* podcast, https://podcasts.apple.com/us/podcast/the-storychanger/id1581826891.

# Introduction to *Exodus: Stories of Redemption and Relationship*

Exodus tells the story of how God redeemed Israel, entered a covenant relationship with Israel, and provided laws to keep that relationship holy, healthy, and happy.

It commences with redemption by God, climaxes in relationship with God, and continues with moral and religious guidelines that ensure a loving, worshipful friendship with God.

As Moses wrote of Christ (see John 5:46; Luke 24:27, 44), Exodus points to how we are redeemed by Christ, brought into a loving relationship with Christ, and guided into greater enjoyment of Christ (see John 14:15–21).

May these stories of redemption and relationship change our stories and make us storytellers so that we become storychangers too.

God uses weak people to fulfill his strong promises.

Hear God's Story | Change Your Story | Tell the Story | Change Others' Stories

1

# God's Unbreakable Promise to the Broken

## EXODUS 1:1–22

Hard times in God's providence make it hard to trust God's promises. Sometimes we feel broken and God's promises feel broken. We lose a loved one, we're diagnosed with cancer, our daughter's marriage is failing, a friend betrays us, our church is shrinking. And it's only Monday. Hard times in God's providence make it hard to trust God's promises.

*How can we trust God's unbreakable promises when they seem to be broken?* In Exodus 1, God gives us three helps to trust his promises in tough providences.

### God's Promise Is Fulfilled in Surprising Ways 1:1–7

Exodus 1 opens with God's people in Egypt, far from the land God had promised them. Due to famine, the Israelites ended up living in Egypt, where Joseph, his brothers, and the rest of that generation of leaders died (1:1–6).

What a disaster! Despite God's repeated promise to Abraham, Isaac, and Jacob of a multiplied people in the promised land, they are doomed to die in a pagan land.

This is a situation ripe for a heavenly "but," which God sovereignly provides: "But the people of Israel were fruitful and increased greatly; they multiplied and grew exceedingly strong, so that the land was filled with them" (1:7).

*God keeps his promises, even when we can't keep our faith.*

*"So, they all lived happily ever after?"*
*No, God's promise is always opposed.*

## God's Promise Is Always Opposed 1:8–14

Israel was growing but so was opposition. The new Pharaoh had hard thoughts toward Israel, imposed hard bosses on Israel, and demanded hard work from Israel (1:8–12). "They ruthlessly made the people of Israel work as slaves and made their lives bitter with hard service. . . . In all their work they ruthlessly made them work as slaves" (1:13–14).

***God's promises will be battered, but they will never be broken.***

*"So does God raise up a mighty leader at this point?"*
*Sometimes, but not always.*

## God's Promise Uses Weak People 1:15–21

God's promise overcomes this opposition by continuing to multiply Israel (1:12). Pharaoh therefore commands the midwives to murder all Hebrew baby boys as they are born (1:15–16), another desperate turn of events. Surely now Israel is finished, the Messianic line is terminated, salvation is lost, and the devil is victorious. If only there were another powerful person like Joseph to deliver them.

Instead, God went to the other end of the scale. He used Hebrew midwives to protect his people and his gospel: "But the midwives feared God and did not do as the king of Egypt commanded them, but let the male children live" (1:17). As a result of their courageous faith, God protected the midwives from Pharaoh and provided families for them (1:18–22).

***God uses weak people to fulfill his strong promises.***

## Changing Our Story with God's Story

God established patterns in the Old Testament narratives to prepare God's national son, Israel, for God's eternal Son, Jesus. From reading this story, what would Israel be primed to expect in God's future Story? They would expect God's promise to be fulfilled in surprising ways, God's promise to be opposed, and God's promise to be fulfilled using weak people.

That's the pattern we see repeatedly in the Old Testament. But nowhere do we see it more clearly than in God's climactic story of Jesus. God kept his promises in the most surprising way in the birth of Jesus to a poor family. God's promise was so opposed that it culminated in Jesus's murder. But Jesus defeated all opposition through the weakness of death and then used weak disciples to fulfill his promises in the New Testament church. Surprise, opposition, and weakness is God's promise pattern. This Story can become our story too.

**Summary:** How can I trust God's unbreakable promises when they seem to be broken? *Strengthen your faith by remembering that God's normal pattern of promise-keeping is surprise, opposition, and weakness.*

**Question:** Which broken person can you bring God's unbreakable promises to?

**Prayer:** Promise-Making, Promise-Keeping God, repair my brokenness with your unbreakable promises.

**Faith makes the impossible possible because it's in the God who makes the impossible possible.**

Hear God's Story | Change Your Story | Tell the Story | Change Others' Stories

2

# Faith Makes the Impossible Possible

EXODUS 2:1–10

"It's impossible!" Ever said that? Ever felt that? I have—many times—and I'm sure you have too. God brings us into impossible situations and calls us to face impossible challenges. Perhaps God is challenging you with cancer, or singleness, or loneliness, or depression, or a family conflict, or a career change, or a calling to ministry, or a mission opportunity. Whatever our predicament, we despond and say, "It's impossible!"

Why does God do this? *Why does God ask us to do the impossible?* Let's answer this by observing how Moses's parents responded to God's impossible challenge in Exodus 2:1–10.

## Faith Obeys God More Than People 2:1–2

The king of Egypt issued an edict that all Israelite boys were to be thrown into the Nile. But Moses's parents knew that the King of kings had issued another edict, to preserve and protect life. Two kings. Two opposing decrees. It was an impossible situation.

What did they do? They hid baby Moses from the king of Egypt, one of the most outstanding acts of faith in the Bible. "By faith Moses, when he was born, was hidden for three months by his parents, because they saw that the child was beautiful, and they were not afraid of the king's edict" (Heb. 11:23). Faith enabled Moses's dad and mom to obey a holy God rather than an evil person, and God memorialized their faith for all people for all time in the Bible's hall of faith.

***We may never get in the hall of fame,***
***but we can get into the hall of faith.***

*"Can faith take away the horrible feelings of helplessness?"*
*Yes, as Moses's parents demonstrate.*

## Faith Hopes More Than Despairs 2:3–4

After three months, Moses's parents realized they couldn't hide him any longer. It was impossible. But instead of giving him up to the authorities to be killed, they gave him up to God for protection. They put him in a basket and floated him down the Nile and trusted that God could make this river of death a river of life.

***Faith doesn't give up on God but gives over to God.***

*"What can we expect if we trust God?"*
*We can expect to get more than we can imagine.*

## Faith Receives More Than It Expects 2:4–10

Baby Moses was floating down a baby-killing river when the king of Egypt's daughter arrived and found him. Of all people! It was an impossible situation. But God put pity in her Egyptian heart. She realized it was a Hebrew boy doomed to die and adopted him as her son.

At this point Moses's big sister, Miriam, jumped in and offered to find a Hebrew mother to nurse the baby. The princess agreed and paid their mother to nurse baby Moses! The river of death became a river of life and the murderous king's daughter became the savior of the King of kings' son!

The princess even gave him the name *Moses*, meaning "drawn out." This was a description of what she did for him, but in God's design it was also a prediction of the redemption he would accomplish for Israel from Egypt.

***Faith makes the impossible possible because it's in the God who makes the impossible possible.***

## Changing Our Story with God's Story

Is anything too hard for our God? No, as the King's special Son said, "What is impossible with man is possible with God" (Luke 18:27). Jesus, the greater Moses, the greater Drawn-Out, drew his people out of bondage. He is still redeeming, still drawing us out of bondage.

**Summary:** Why does God ask us to do the impossible? *God asks us to do the impossible to strengthen our faith in the one who can make the impossible possible.*

**Question:** What impossible situation are you facing? How will this passage help you out of your helplessness?

**Prayer:** God of the Impossible, strengthen my faith in you through the impossible challenges you bring into my life for my good.

**Son-glasses help us see God's people in a new light.**

3

# Change Your Glasses to Change Your Choices

EXODUS 2:11–15

How would you like to make thirty-five thousand decisions a day? Believe it or not, you already do! Some of these are simple choices that require virtually no thought (e.g., ice cream or broccoli?). Others are far more consequential and costly.

Sometimes, for example, we must choose between Christ's people and worldly people. That shouldn't be a difficult choice, but it can be. Standing with Christ's people often involves shame, suffering, and loss. Do I really want to choose that?

*How do we make the right spiritual choices regardless of consequences?* Moses can help us here because when he had to make the biggest spiritual choice of his life, he chose Christ's people over Egyptians. He chose shame, suffering, and loss instead of status, pleasures, and riches.

How did he do that? He changed his choices by changing his glasses. He put on Son-glasses. When he saw Christ by faith, he saw things differently and chose rightly. That's how Hebrews 11:24–26 explains Exodus 2:11–15. Let's pick up these Son-glasses and see what Moses saw.

## Faith Chooses Christ's People over Royal Families 2:11–15

Moses was raised in Egypt and was a member of the royal family. But when he saw an Egyptian boss abusing an Israelite slave, he knew he was at a fork in the road. He could side with the Egyptian boss and keep his royal status, or he could intervene on behalf of the Israelite slave and lose his royal status.

That's when Moses put on his Son-glasses and saw everything differently. Instead of seeing an abused Israelite slave, he saw a child of the King of kings, and so chose God's royal people over Egyptian royalty. As Hebrews 11:24 puts it: "By faith Moses, when he was grown up, refused to be called the son of Pharaoh's daughter." He made the right choice, although in killing the Egyptian, he went about this part of it in the wrong way.

***Son-glasses help us see God's people in a new light.***

*"But won't that result in suffering?"*
*Yes, and that's where we need our Son-glasses again.*

## Faith Chooses Christ's Suffering over Sinful Pleasures **Heb. 11:25**

Hebrews 11:25 helps us see inside Moses's thought processes when he put on his Son-glasses. We see him "choosing rather to be mistreated with the people of God than to enjoy the fleeting pleasures of sin." His Son-glasses enabled him to see more glory in suffering with Christ's people than in enjoying Egyptian pleasures and popularity.

***Son-glasses help us to see the beauty of suffering for Christ.***

*"What did faith see that helped Moses make those choices?"*
*Moses saw the reward at the end of the road.*

## Faith Chooses Christ's Reward over Earth's Treasures **Heb. 11:26**

"He considered the reproach of Christ greater wealth than the treasures of Egypt, for he was looking to the reward" (Heb 11:26).

Moses compared the wages—reproach of Christ or riches of Egypt—and chose Christ's wages even though it involved financial loss. But we know why he did this. By faith Moses saw the gain of the final wage packet, which would more than compensate for all the previous losses.

*Son-glasses help us to see the reward at the end of the road.*

### Changing Our Story with God's Story

Praise God for giving us these Son-glasses. Without them, we wouldn't see clearly enough to make the right choices. Praise God for his Son who had perfect vision. By faith, he chose God's way over the devil's way. By faith he chose shame, suffering, and loss over worldly status, pleasures, and rewards. Or, to put it positively, he chose heavenly status, pleasures, and rewards over worldly status, pleasures, and rewards.

**Summary:** How do we make the right spiritual choices regardless of consequences? *Use Son-glasses to choose Christ's shame, sufferings, and losses and gain heavenly status, pleasures, and rewards.*

**Question:** How have you used these Son-glasses to change your past choices, and how will you use them to change your present choices?

**Prayer:** All-Seeing Optician, give me Son-glasses so that I can make right spiritual choices regardless of the consequences.

**When we can't get up, God comes down.**

Hear God's Story | Change Your Story | Tell the Story | Change Others' Stories

# 4

# God Comes Down to Lift You Up

## EXODUS 3:1–12

Have you ever felt down-and-out? So down-and-out that you've thought you'll never be up-and-in again? You had great hopes and dreams, but now you feel like a nobody, doing a nothing job, with a nothing future. Life is hard, worship is cold, loneliness is your only friend. You're down-and-out. *How do we get up-and-in when we're down-and-out?* I've asked that question more than once in my life. Moses is my favorite elevator.

No one was more down and out than Moses. Turn to Exodus 3:1–12, and watch as God helps him up-and-in again.

### God Saves by Coming Down in Unexpected Ways 3:1–6

It's been forty years since Moses fled from Egypt in Exodus 2. He was a prince in Egypt, and now he's a poor shepherd in the desert (3:1). But God comes down at the most unexpected time and in the most unexpected way. "And the angel of the Lord appeared to him in a flame of fire out of the midst of a bush. He looked, and behold, the bush was burning, yet it was not consumed" (3:2).

Moses thinks this is a great sight but doesn't realize at first that it is a God-sight. As he turns to inspect this strange bush, God speaks to him out of it: "'Do not come near; take your sandals off your feet, for the place on which you are standing is holy ground.' And he said, 'I am the God of your father, the God of Abraham, the God of Isaac, and the God of Jacob.' And Moses hid his face, for he was afraid to look at God" (3:5–6).

***When we can't get up, God comes down.***

*"How is God going to do this saving?"*
*God has a surprising plan.*

## God Saves by Sending a Go-Between 3:7–10

Moses had asked many times, "Does God know his people are suffering?" God answers, "I have surely seen the affliction of my people who are in Egypt and have heard their cry because of their taskmasters. I know their sufferings" (3:7). He's coming down to lift his people up out of Egypt and into the promised land (3:8–9).

At this point, Moses is sitting back saying, "Great, I can't wait to see this!" But God says, "Come, I will send you to Pharaoh that you may bring my people, the children of Israel, out of Egypt" (3:10). These are the last words Moses expected to hear. Instead of "Come, watch me deliver Israel," it's "Come, I will send you to deliver Israel." God saves through a go-between.

***When everything's broken, God sends a broker.***

*"What's God's aim in sending this broker or mediator?"*
*His purpose in saving people is to lift up the down-and-out.*

## God Saves the Down-and-Out for Liftoff 3:11–12

God assures Moses, "When you have brought the people out of Egypt, you shall serve God on this mountain" (3:12). When God lifts Israel's burdens, Israel will lift off in worship.

***God takes the down-and-out and makes them up-and-in.***

## Changing Our Story with God's Story

Where do these truths lead us? They lead us to Christ, the greater Moses. He saved by coming down in unexpected ways. He saved by becoming the go-between. He saves the down-and-out for liftoff. We love Moses for what he did, but we have a greater love for the greater Moses because of his greater doing.

**Summary:** How do we get up-and-in when we're down-and-out? *Ask Jesus to come down by his Spirit to save the down-and-out and lift us up-and-in.*

**Question:** Who do you know that is down-and-out and how will you bring this uplifting message to them?

**Prayer:** Greater-Than-Moses, you can lift those who are most down-and-out and take them higher and closer to you than even Moses did. Thank you for doing that for me. Use me to do it in others' lives too.

**When we remember God's name, we reconnect with God's power.**

5

# What a Powerful Name It Is!

**EXODUS 3:13–22**

One of my weaknesses is forgetting people's names—a bad weakness for a pastor to have. Remembering names means a lot to people as it strengthens our relationship with them. Forgetting fades friendships; remembering reinforces relationships.

The same is true in the spiritual realm. In Exodus 3, we find Israel suffering from spiritual amnesia. They have forgotten God's name, leaving them feeble and fragile.

God's name can fade from our minds too, weakening and undermining our relationship with him. *How do we recover from this spiritual weakness?* In verses 13–22, Moses directs Israel and us to God's name. We rebuild our relationship by remembering God's name.

## God's Name Is Memorable 3:13–15

Once Moses gets over the shock of God choosing him to save Israel from Egypt, he anticipates his first conversation with Israel in Egypt: "If I come to the people of Israel and say to them, 'The God of your fathers has sent me to you,' and they ask me, 'What is his name?' what shall I say to them?" (3:13). Moses knew that after four hundred years in Egypt, Israel will have forgotten the God of Israel. "Who? What's his name? Who's that?" he hears them asking.

What answer does God give Moses? "God said to Moses, 'I AM WHO I AM.' And he said, 'Say this to the people of Israel: "I AM has sent me to you." . . . This is my name forever, and thus I am to be remembered throughout all generations'" (3:14–15).

God reaches into the dark attics of their minds and helps them find dusty recollections from their dim and distant past. As he wipes the dust off his name, he essentially says, "You've forgotten my name, so let me help you remember it. It is 'I AM WHO I AM.' Who I was to your fathers I am to you. I was who I was, I am who I was, I was who I am, I am who I am, and I am who I will be."

"This is my name forever, and thus I am to be remembered throughout all generations."

***How can we forget God's unforgettable name?***

*"But what does remembering God's name do?"*
*It recharges flat spiritual batteries.*

## God's Name Is Powerful 3:16–22

Moses is to tell Israel that God has seen Israel's powerlessness and will flex his muscles for them. "I have observed you and what has been done to you in Egypt, and I promise that I will bring you up out of the affliction of Egypt to . . . a land flowing with milk and honey" (3:16–17).

But a powerful promise is weak unless it is believed. Will they or won't they believe? "And they will listen to your voice" (3:18), and they will demand that the king of Egypt let them go. Although the king will oppose this (3:19), God promises a powerful deliverance: "So I will stretch out my hand and strike Egypt with all the wonders that I will do in it; after that he will let you go" (3:20).

***When we remember God's name,***
***we reconnect with God's power.***

### Changing Our Story with God's Story

When Jesus came to deliver us from our sins, he said, "Truly, truly, I say to you, before Abraham was, I am" (John 8:58). He also made a number of other "I am" statements (e.g., John 6:35; 8:12; 10:9, 11). He promised great power through his name: "If you ask anything in my name, I will do it" (John 14:14). The apostles made Christ's name known: "There is no other name under heaven given among men by which we must be saved" (Acts 4:12; see Rom. 10:13). What a memorable name! What a powerful name! The name of Jesus.

**Summary:** How do we recover from spiritual weakness? *Remember, believe, and call upon God's name to experience an empowering relationship with God and enjoy powerful deliverances by God.*

**Question:** What can you do to remind yourself of this empowering name of God?

**Prayer:** Unforgettable God, strengthen my soul by strengthening my memory of your powerful and empowering name.

**Doubt is a weed multiplier, but faith is a weed killer.**

6

# God's Compassion for Doubters

EXODUS 4:1–17

The weed of doubt never grows alone. When we plant the seed of doubt in God's word or God's power, the weeds of fear, disobedience, and pessimism also take root and grow. Very soon our soul is overgrown and choked with these ugly weeds. *Which gardener can uproot our doubt and replant our souls with faith?* Let's visit the field of Exodus 4:1–17 where God digs deep into Moses's soul to uproot doubt and replant faith.

## God Will Crush the Serpent's Head 4:2–5

Moses feared that when he told Israel God had sent him to deliver them from Egypt, they wouldn't believe him (4:1). God therefore gave Moses a sign to prove his claims. Moses's staff turned into a snake and then turned back into a staff when Moses was persuaded to pick it up (4:3–4). God assured Moses that when Israel saw his power over the snake, they would "believe that the Lord, the God of their fathers, the God of Abraham, the God of Isaac, and the God of Jacob, has appeared to you" (4:5). God used the serpent as a servant to grow faith in the Israelites, by reminding them of his promises to defeat the serpent in Genesis 3:15.

*The serpent-crusher is the devil-crusher.*

*"God can kill our killer, but can he give us life?"*
*That's what the next sign points us to.*

## God Will Give Life to the Dead 4:6–8

God then gave Moses a second sign to prove his claims. He turned Moses's hand leprous but then removed the leprosy. "'If they will not believe you,' God said, 'or listen to the first sign, they may believe the latter sign'" (4:8). Leprosy meant death, but God would give life to their faith by demonstrating his power to give life to the dead.

***Doubt is a weed multiplier, but faith is a weed killer.***

*"Will God do this for everyone?"*
*The river of blood says no.*

## God Will Judge the World 4:9

Because Israel's doubt was so deep-rooted, God gave Moses a third sign, that of turning the River Nile into blood (4:9). The Nile was the life of Egypt, so much so that the Egyptians worshiped it. But God would judge their source of life by turning it to blood. It was a warning to Israel that God would judge those who are not his people. There would be life for his people but death for the world.

***God can turn life into blood and blood into life.***

*"How does God get this message out?"*
*In the least expected way.*

## God Uses Weak Servants 4:10–17

Unsurprisingly Moses was terrified by the prospect of this and essentially said, "I'm no speaker. I can't do that" (4:10). "Then the LORD said to him, 'Who has made man's mouth? Who makes him mute, or deaf, or seeing, or blind? Is it not I, the LORD? Now therefore go, and I will be with your mouth and teach you what you shall speak'" (4:11–12). When Moses continued to object, God agreed to Moses using Aaron as his spokesperson (4:13–16). God didn't give up on Moses but gave him help to strengthen his faith.

*Our powerful God speaks through powerless servants.*

## Changing Our Story with God's Story

I love God's patient gardening here. It was a tough battle with deep weeds, but God eventually uprooted doubt from Moses's heart and replaced it with faith. In doing so, he also removed fear, disobedience, and pessimism and planted encouragement, power, and hope. Praise God for his gardening skill, and that he can turn the most overgrown and weed-infested soul into a garden paradise of faith and trust. Let's use these miracles to turn our dangerous jungles into botanic gardens.

**Summary:** Which gardener can uproot our doubt and replant our souls with faith? *God can uproot the deepest dandelions of doubt and replant with the most beautiful flowers of faith.*

**Question:** Which weed of doubt is growing in your soul? Which truth of God can dig it out?

**Prayer:** My Gardener, find and extract every doubting weed in my soul and plant instead the flowers of faith for my good and your pleasure.

**The devil may win some battles, but he's losing the war.**

Hear God's Story | Change Your Story | Tell the Story | Change Others' Stories

7

# His Rage We Can Endure, for Lo, His Doom Is Sure

EXODUS 5

Do you ever feel the devil seems to be winning? We look out at the world, we see his defiant, destructive, and divisive power, and we worry, "Is the devil going to win?" We look at our lives or our family's lives and ask, *"Is the devil going to win?"*

The Bible assures us that despite his horrendous power the devil is actually a defeated enemy. In Exodus 5, we see the devil's great power in Pharaoh, but we also see his certain defeat in Pharaoh.

## The Devil Is Defiant 5:1–2

When God demanded that Pharaoh release Israel (5:1), Pharaoh disdained God and his command: "Who is the LORD, that I should obey his voice and let Israel go? I do not know the LORD, and moreover, I will not let Israel go" (5:2).

***Defiance is devilish.***

*"How does that defiance work itself out in practice?"*
*The devil goes on the attack to destroy Israel.*

## The Devil Is Destructive 5:3–19

Moses and Aaron persevered and demanded that Pharaoh release Israel to worship God in the wilderness (5:3). Pharaoh responded by making their slavery even harder. "They are idle," said Pharaoh. "Therefore they cry, 'Let us go and offer sacrifice to our God.' Let heavier work be laid on the men that they may labor at it and pay no regard to lying words" (5:8–9). All this talk of religion is distracting you, so let me show you how dangerous and damaging such religious lies are.

***Destruction is devilish.***

*"What is the effect of this destructiveness?"*
*The devil divides the Israelites and Moses.*

## The Devil Is Divisive 5:20–23

"They met Moses and Aaron, who were waiting for them, as they came out from Pharaoh; and they said to them, 'The LORD look on you and judge, because you have made us stink in the sight of Pharaoh and his servants, and have put a sword in their hand to kill us'" (5:20–21).

Having divided Israel and Moses, the devil moves on to dividing Moses from God. "Then Moses turned to the LORD and said, 'O Lord, why have you done evil to this people? Why did you ever send me? For since I came to Pharaoh to speak in your name, he has done evil to this people, and you have not delivered your people at all'" (5:22–23).

***Division is devilish.***

*"If the devil is defiant, destructive, and divisive, what hope is there?"*
*There's great hope for God's people but no hope for the devil.*

## The Devil Is Defeated 6:1

Chapter 6 assures us that his doom is sure. "But the LORD said to Moses, 'Now you shall see what I will do to Pharaoh; for with a strong hand he will send them out, and with a strong hand he will drive them out of his land'" (6:1). God will defeat the devil and deliver his people.

*The devil may win some battles, but he's losing the war.*

### Changing Our Story with God's Story

That last point changes the whole picture, doesn't it? The devil often seems to be winning. Our *eyes* see his defiance, destruction, and division. But our *faith* sees his defeat. As Martin Luther sang, "His rage we can endure, for lo, his doom is sure."[1] We see that pictured here in Pharaoh's doom. We see that for real at the cross. We see it in our own salvation. We see it in every conversion. We will see it at the end of time. How great is our God!

**Summary:** Is the devil going to win? *Despite the devil's powerful opposition, have perfect confidence that he will be defeated.*

**Question:** Where have you seen Satan defeated recently? How does that change how you live today?

**Prayer:** Devil-Defeater, you see the devil's raging attacks upon my life. I'm acutely and painfully aware of his raging defiance, division, and destruction. But you have ensured his defeat. Encourage me to fight him, knowing his doom is sure.

1 "A Mighty Fortress Is Our God," 1529.

**Our commitment to God may turn to sand, but God's commitment to us is uncrackable concrete.**

# 8

# A Concrete Covenant for Sandy Faith

EXODUS 6:1–13

Severe suffering can weaken our faith. When we're in pain, it can be hard to hear and believe the gospel. That's what happened to the Israelites in Egyptian slavery. "Moses spoke thus to the people of Israel, but they did not listen to Moses, because of their broken spirit and harsh slavery" (Ex. 6:9). *How do we strengthen our suffering-weakened faith?* Let's see how God helped Israel so we can get help too.

## The Covenant Maker Reveals His Covenant Commitment 6:1–4

God began by revealing his covenant strength. "But the Lord said to Moses, 'Now you shall see what I will do to Pharaoh; for with a strong hand he will send them out, and with a strong hand he will drive them out of his land'" (6:1). God says, "Your grip on me may be weak but my grip on you is strong."

Then God revealed his covenant name. "I am the Lord. I appeared to Abraham, to Isaac, and to Jacob, as God Almighty, but by my name the Lord I did not make myself known to them" (6:2–3). God had used this name in the past to confirm his covenant commitments. But the level of God's commitment to his covenant people was about to be revealed in such a new way that it would be as if Israel had never heard it before.

***God's name doesn't change, but our experience of it does.***

*"We forget our promises. Does God forget his?"*
*Never.*

## The Covenant Maker Remembers His Covenant Commitment 6:5–6

God's covenant name, "the Lord," means "I am committed to redeem you." "I am the Lord, and I will bring you out from under the burdens of the Egyptians, and I will deliver you from slavery to them, and I will redeem you with an outstretched arm and with great acts of judgment" (6:5–6). When God remembers his name, it's not that he ever forgot it; it's that his next actions are based on it and will flow from it. Because God committed to Israel's redemption in the past, God is irreversibly committed to Israel in the present.

***We can forget our commitment to God,***
***but God never forgets his commitment to us.***

*"Sometimes I need reassurance."*
*Will God give me that when I need it?*

## The Covenant Maker Reassures Us of His Covenant Commitment 6:7–13

God reassured Israel of his commitment to this relationship. "I will take you to be my people, and I will be your God, and you shall know that I am the Lord your God, who has brought you out from under the burdens of the Egyptians" (6:7).

But despite God's concrete commitment, Israel's pain-weakened faith had turned to sand. "Moses spoke thus to the people of Israel, but they did not listen to Moses, because of their broken spirit and harsh slavery" (6:9).

At this point Israel's weak faith infected Moses too. "Behold, the people of Israel have not listened to me. How then shall Pharaoh listen to me?" (6:12). Israel's commitment is sand, Moses's commitment is sand, but God's commitment is concrete. "But the Lord spoke to Moses and Aaron and gave them a charge about the people of Israel and about Pharaoh king of Egypt: to bring the people of Israel out of the land of Egypt" (6:13).

*Our commitment to God may turn to sand,*
*but God's commitment to us is uncrackable concrete.*

## Changing Our Story with God's Story

We worship the Lord of concrete commitment, the Lord of unbreakable resolve, the Lord of irreversible relationship. We worship the Lord who uses our times of suffering to reveal his shatterproof engagement to us in a whole new way. When severe suffering weakens our faith in God's covenant, let's use Christ's covenant suffering to strengthen our faith in God's covenant.

**Summary:** How do we strengthen our suffering-weakened faith? *Use God's concrete commitment to cement your sandy faith.*

**Question:** Whose sandy faith will you strengthen with God's covenant concrete today?

**Prayer:** Covenant Maker, suffering has turned my spirituality to sand. Pour your concrete covenant into my life so that I can be strengthened and become a strengthener of others.

**If we're hardened to God, we'll be hardened to people.**

Hear God's Story | Change Your Story | Tell the Story | Change Others' Stories

# 9

# Hardness Makes It Harder

## EXODUS 7

A hardened heart is a hell-bound heart. How does that happen? It happens when, instead of listening to and learning from God's word, God's power, and God's judgments, we are deaf to them and dismiss them.

When Pharaoh hardened his heart to God's word, God's power, and God's judgments in Exodus 7, God punished him with more hardening. The hardening got worse and worse, until eventually Pharaoh was as sensitive as a stone to suffering. *How do we get and keep a soft heart?* Let's view the alarming impact of a hardened heart with a view to ensuring the opposite happens to us.

### A Hard Heart Dismisses God's Word 7:1–7

Having commissioned Moses to speak God's word to Pharaoh, God confirmed Moses's fear that Pharaoh would not listen. Yes, says God, "I will harden Pharaoh's heart, and . . . Pharaoh will not listen to you" (7:3–4). That's exactly what happened (see 7:13–14). God's word was dismissed and Pharaoh's heart was hardened. It was a vicious circle. Pharaoh hardened his heart against God's word and therefore God hardened Pharaoh against his word, which in turn made Pharaoh harden his heart . . . and so on.

*When God's word doesn't soften us,*
*it hardens us.*

*"Pharaoh won't listen to the word of God,*
*but surely he'll listen to the wonders of God?"*
*Nope, God says, my signs won't do it either.*

## A Hard Heart Dismisses God's Power 7:8–13

When God's power was demonstrated in the wonder of the staff becoming a serpent, Pharaoh's magicians did the same with the devil's power (7:8–12). The result? "Still Pharaoh's heart was hardened, and he would not listen to them, as the LORD had said" (7:13). God's power was dismissed.

***God's power either strengthens our faith or strengthens our sin.***

*"Yes, but if he could see a judgment, he would listen and soften."*
*Let's see what happens.*

## A Hard Heart Dismisses God's Judgments 7:14–25

God judged the Nile by turning it into blood, so that all the fish died, the water stank, and the people couldn't drink it (7:14–21). This would do it, surely. Nope. The magicians did a devilish duplication and "Pharaoh's heart remained hardened, and he would not listen to them, as the LORD had said. Pharaoh turned and went into his house, and he did not take even this to heart" (7:22–23). God's judgment was dismissed.

Pharaoh was hardened not just to God's voice but to human suffering. For the next seven days the thirsty "Egyptians dug along the Nile for water to drink, for they could not drink the water of the Nile" (7:24).

***If we're hardened to God,***
***we'll be hardened to people.***

## Changing Our Story with God's Story

A hard heart dismisses God's word, God's power, and God's judgments.

When we see how hard the human heart can become, how thankful we should be that God has softened, sensitized, and tenderized our hearts.

As I look back on my teens and early twenties, I see myself hardening my heart to God's word, God's power, and God's judgments. I was steely cold to God and others. But God in his massive mercy broke through my thick layers of unbelief and melted my heart. I'm sure many of you have similar stories of grace. Let's sing songs to the Sinner Softener.

**Summary:** How do we get and keep a soft heart? *Be sensitive and responsive to God's word, power, and judgments to soften and sensitize your heart to God's voice and human suffering.*

**Question:** What is the greatest potential heart hardener in your life?

**Prayer:** Your word, O God, is a sinner softener or a heart hardener. Please give me a soft heart so that I am sensitive and responsive to you and others.

**Pandemics are powerful, but God's finger is more powerful.**

Hear God's Story | Change Your Story | Tell the Story | Change Others' Stories

10

# Are Plagues and Pandemics the Finger of God?

## EXODUS 8

Can a particular plague or pandemic be the judgment of God on a sinful world? Many Christians say, "No, God's not like that; a pandemic is just something that comes round every hundred years or so." Others say, "It's a massive judgment from God that can bring the world to repentance and result in a great revival." *What's the right way to view and use pandemics?* No judgment, or big salvation?

The plagues in Exodus 8 have much to teach us about how to view modern-day plagues in a balanced, biblical way.

### God's Judgments Magnify Him 8:1–15

When Pharaoh pled with Moses to remove the plague of frogs, Moses replied, "Be it as you say, so that you may know that there is no one like the LORD our God. The frogs shall go away from you and your houses and your servants and your people" (8:10–11). Moses used God's judgment to magnify God's uniqueness. There is no one like him. He is incomparable in his truth and his power. "And the LORD did according to the word of Moses. The frogs died out in the houses, the courtyards, and the fields" (8:13). God's judgments magnified his truth and his power.

*Pandemics magnify God and shrink us.*

*"I love that God's judgments lift God high, but I also want to see evil brought low." Watch this.*

## God's Judgments Defeat Evil 8:16–19

Up to this point, the Egyptian magicians had been able to duplicate God's wonders, but now their power has run out. The magicians try to produce gnats but can't. "Then the magicians said to Pharaoh, 'This is the finger of God.' But Pharaoh's heart was hardened, and he would not listen to them, as the LORD had said" (8:19). God's judgments were more powerful than evil's efforts.

***Pandemics are powerful, but God's finger is more powerful.***

*"How can I be sure God's judgments will not spill over and impact me too?" You don't need to worry.*

## God's Judgments Are Targeted 8:20–24

God next showed his power not only by targeting the Egyptians with a plague of flies but by protecting his people from them. "On that day I will set apart the land of Goshen, where my people dwell, so that no swarms of flies shall be there, that you may know that I am the LORD in the midst of the earth. Thus I will put a division between my people and your people. . . . And the LORD did so" (8:22–24). God's judgments are not scattershot but precision shot.

***A pandemic is laser-guided by God and causes no collateral damage.***

*"Does that mean I should pray for God's judgments so that the wicked turn to Christ?" Yes, but judgment alone won't do it.*

## God's Judgments Do Not Save 8:25–32

Now Pharaoh started negotiating with Moses: "OK, you can sacrifice to God but only within Egypt." Moses said no (8:25–27). "OK, you can sacrifice in the wilderness but not far away. And, by the way, pray for me" (8:28). Moses took that deal but warned Pharaoh not to cheat and change his mind (8:29). That's exactly what Pharaoh did though. As soon as Moses had removed every last fly from Egypt, "Pharaoh hardened his heart this time also, and did not let the people go" (8:32). God's judgments had a short-term impact on Pharaoh, but not a saving impact.

*Pandemics can change behavior,*
*but only the gospel can change the heart.*

### Changing Our Story with God's Story

We stand in awe at the power of God's judgments and the power of God's patience. Whether it's Egyptian plagues or a worldwide pandemic, we are humbled by God's awesome power and awesome patience. As we are humbled and silenced, we ask God how to use plagues and pandemics for our good and the good of others.

**Summary:** What's the right way to view a pandemic? *Use such times to believe the gospel and commend Jesus as the world's only hope of salvation.*

**Question:** How has God used modern-day plagues and pandemics for good in your life? How have you used modern-day plagues and pandemics for good in others' lives?

**Prayer:** Just Judge, I bow in awe before your holy judgments and ask that you will use them to exalt you, defeat evil, humble me, and open ears to the gospel.

# The wicked make their plans, but God has the master plan.

Hear God's Story | Change Your Story | Tell the Story | Change Others' Stories

11

# God's Purpose for the Wicked

## EXODUS 9

Why did God let Satan fall from being an angel to becoming the devil? Why didn't God just kill him there and then? Why does God let him and his wicked followers have so much power and success in the world?

If we haven't asked these questions ourselves, we've surely been asked them by others. In some ways, these are impossible questions to answer. We're left feeling stumped and have to reluctantly admit, "I just don't know," which doesn't seem to help us or anyone else who's asking. Is there a way to move from helpless ignorance to helpful truth?

God's treatment of wicked Pharaoh in Exodus 9 provides some helpful answers—though probably not all the answers—to these awkward and challenging questions about God's purpose for the wicked and especially the wicked one. Let's ask Exodus 9, *How can we find spiritual help in God's purpose for the wicked?*

### God Has a Purpose for the Wicked 9:13–16

Plagues 1–6 only hardened Pharaoh's heart harder (9:7, 12). When God sent Moses to announce the seventh plague to Pharaoh, he also gave him a minisermon to preach (9:13–19). God's first point was *I'm bigger and better than you* (9:14). His second point was *I can kill you at any moment* (9:15). His third point was *I'm using you*: "But for this purpose I have raised you up, to show you my power, so that my name may be proclaimed in all the earth" (9:16). God raises the wicked up for a purpose and keeps them alive for a purpose.

***The wicked make their plans, but God has the master plan.***

*"What is God's purpose for the wicked?"*
*To show his power in the wicked.*

## God Shows His Power in the Wicked 9:16

God didn't leave Pharaoh in the dark about what his purpose was. It was to show his power to the wicked and to show his power through the wicked: "For this purpose I have raised you up, to show you my power, so that my name may be proclaimed in all the earth" (9:16). Or as Paul put it, "For this very purpose I have raised you up, that I might show my power in you" (Rom. 9:17). God shows his power to, in, and through the wicked.

***The wicked are powerful, but God is all-powerful.***

*"Is that God's sole purpose—just to show his power?"*
*No, it's also to get more praise.*

## God Is Praised through the Wicked 9:16

There was no name like Pharaoh's in the ancient world. His name was known everywhere and praised everywhere. But God replaced Pharaoh's name with his own. I'm doing all this, God says, "so that my name may be proclaimed in all the earth" (9:16). Pharaoh, your name will be expunged and eradicated, but my name will be proclaimed and praised.

***The wicked's names are fading, but God's name will be famous.***

## Changing Our Story with God's Story

Let's honor our God by delighting in his triumphant purpose, his victorious power, and his peerless name. His purpose, power, and name will conquer *the* wicked one and all wicked ones.

We see this in Moses's confrontation with wicked Pharaoh, and we see it even more stunningly in Christ's confrontation with the devil during his life and in his death. There, in mile-high capital letters, we behold God's triumphant purpose, his victorious power, and his peerless name. There, we hear Christ's answer to all these questions about the devil: "I'm showing the world that I'm bigger and better than you, that I can defeat you at any moment, and that I'm using you to advance and achieve my plan."

**Summary:** How can we find spiritual help in God's purpose for the wicked? *Use the wicked to rejoice in God's triumphant purpose, victorious power, and peerless name.*

**Question:** How can you change your view of the wicked so that they become a help to your spiritual life?

**Prayer:** Powerful and Purposeful God, show me your purpose for the wicked by showing me your power over the wicked, so that I praise your name more. Amen.

**God doesn't bargain with sinners. In the gospel, he offers sinners a bargain.**

Hear God's Story | Change Your Story | Tell the Story | Change Others' Stories

12

# Faker, Fighter, or Faith

EXODUS 10

Hard things from God can produce hard thoughts about God. When God sends hard things into our lives, we often react badly. We try to bargain with God, we fake repentance, we take our frustrations out on God and his people. That's exactly how Pharaoh reacted to God's judgments in Exodus 10.

*How should we respond to hard things from God?* Let's look at Pharaoh's wrong responses so that we can learn a better and safer way.

## We Bargain with God 10:8–15, 21–26

After seven terrible plagues, Pharaoh realized what he was up against, and he started negotiating. His first offer to Moses was, "OK, the men can go and worship God in the wilderness, but leave your children here" (10:8–11). Moses rejected this offer. "No, we must all go and worship God" (10:9).

A couple of plagues later, Pharaoh made his second offer. "OK, you can all go, but leave your animals behind" (10:24). Moses rejected this offer too, because God sets nonnegotiable terms for any deal.

*God doesn't bargain with sinners.*
*In the gospel, he offers sinners a bargain.*

*"Bargaining didn't work for Pharaoh, so what did he try next?"*
*What we often try, too—fake repentance.*

## We Fake Repentance 10:16–20

After the plague of locusts, "Pharaoh hastily called Moses and Aaron and said, 'I have sinned against the LORD your God, and against you. Now therefore, forgive my sin, please, only this once, and plead with the LORD your God only to remove this death from me'" (10:16–17). Pharaoh confessed his sin, asked for forgiveness for one sin, and requested prayer to remove his pain.

This looked promising, but as soon as God removed the plague of locusts, Pharaoh hardened his heart and refused to let Israel go (10:18–20).

***Fake faith is foolish faith and never fools God.***

*"When fake faith didn't work, what did Pharaoh do?"*
*He did what many do: he lashed out at God's people.*

## We Lash Out at God's People 10:27–29

Surely Pharaoh will give up and give in now? Nope. After the next plague, the plague of darkness, Pharaoh drove Moses and Aaron out of his palace and threatened them with death. "Then Pharaoh said to him, 'Get away from me; take care never to see my face again, for on the day you see my face you shall die'" (10:28).

***When people can't attack God, they attack his people.***

## Changing Our Story with God's Story

Aren't you amazed at the patience of God? Yes, in this chapter, we've seen great judgments on Egypt and Pharaoh. But we've also seen God's incredible patience. He could have wiped Pharaoh and Egypt off the face of the planet in a moment. But instead he gives ten opportunities to repent. Pharaoh tries bargaining, he fakes faith, and he attacks God's people, and God still lets him live!

Many of us can look back on our lives and see the same divine patience. How many opportunities did God give us to repent? Many times we tried bargaining, we faked repentance, and we turned on God's people, especially when he sent hard things into our lives. But still he kept offering his terms of peace. Thank God he never gave up on us and that he finally softened us rather than hardened us.

Let's worship the Lord Jesus Christ, who suffered the hardest of judgments yet responded with complete, sincere, and peaceful submission.

**Summary:** How should we respond to hard things from God? When God sends hard things into our lives, let's not bargain, fake it, or go on the attack. *Rather let's submit completely, sincerely, and peacefully, and we'll be safe not sorry.*

**Question:** What hard thing has God brought into your life and how can you improve your response?

**Prayer:** Lord, when you test me with hard things, help me to respond with complete, sincere, and peaceful obedience so that I will be safe not sorry.

**God gives saving grace to his people by giving his goodness to all people.**

13

# God's Everywhere Goodness Serves Particular Grace

**EXODUS 11**

Some unbelievers are better people than some Christians. I've had neighbors who were kinder and gentler than many Christians. Indeed, their generosity has put me to shame at times too. I've heard young Christians tell me that their lesbian or gay colleagues and fellow students are really nice people, nicer than most Christians they know.

That's challenging and perplexing. It also raises some hard questions: Are unbelievers as bad and as doomed as the Bible says? Are believers as saved and as secure as the Bible says? *Is there any difference between Christians and non-Christians?*

A lot of confusion and unbelief can result from these questions. Exodus 11 answers some of them, clarifies our thinking, and strengthens our faith.

## God's Everywhere Goodness Serves His People 11:1–3

Exodus 11 opens with God telling Moses that after one more plague Pharaoh will give Israel freedom (11:1), the Egyptians will give Israel their silver and gold jewelry, the Egyptians will give Israel favor, and the Egyptians will give Moses respect (11:2–3). But as verse 3 reminds us, it's really God behind all this giving.

God worked good things in Pharaoh's and the Egyptians' hearts for the benefit of his people. Some call this *common grace*, to distinguish it from saving grace. I call it *everywhere goodness*. It's a merciful work of God that puts temporary goodness in human hearts everywhere, for the good of God's people. God's everywhere goodness serves his people, although it never saves anyone. As Jesus said, "He makes his sun rise on the evil and on the good, and sends rain on the just and on the unjust" (Matt. 5:45).

***God gives saving grace to his people by giving his goodness to all people.***

*"So, if everywhere goodness doesn't save anyone, what does?" Particular grace.*

## God's Particular Grace Saves His People 11:4–10

In verses 4–10, the focus changes from God's everywhere goodness for the Egyptians to God's particular grace for the Israelites. Egypt will be judged with the killing of all the firstborn (11:4–6), Israel will be preserved from this plague (11:7), and Israel will be delivered from Egypt (11:8), even though Pharaoh will harden his heart one more time (11:9–10).

God demarcates the massive distinction between Israel and Egypt: "There shall be a great cry throughout all the land of Egypt, such as there has never been, nor ever will be again. But not a dog shall growl against any of the people of Israel, either man or beast, that you may know that the Lord makes a distinction between Egypt and Israel" (11:6–8).

We praise Christ for his particular grace that made a saving distinction between us and others who do not know him. Who made us to differ? God alone. Why? Grace alone.

***God's saving grace is distinctly particular.***

## Changing Our Story with God's Story

We thank God for his everywhere goodness. Although it doesn't save anyone, it makes a massive difference to the world. Without it, the world would become decivilized. It would descend into unprecedented anarchy, violence, cruelty, and evil. If you've ever watched a riot on TV, you've seen what the whole world would look like without God's everywhere goodness. Therefore, every day we walk our streets, drive our roads, work, or shop without being murdered is God's amazing gift of everywhere goodness for the good of his people. But that everywhere goodness should also challenge those of us who have received God's saving goodness to excel in showing God's special goodness to others.

**Summary:** Is there any difference between Christians and non-Christians? *Although non-Christians can live moral lives, that's only because of God's everywhere goodness for the benefit of his people who have received special saving grace.*

**Question:** Where do you see God's everywhere goodness around you in your life?

**Prayer:** Lord, I thank you for your everywhere goodness, which serves me, but I especially thank you for your special grace that saves me.

**For salvation to be by grace alone, it must be received by faith alone.**

14

# An Antidote for Amnesia

## EXODUS 12:1–14

"How did I forget her birthday?" What man hasn't asked that question, at least once in his life?

But how about, "How did I forget my salvation?" It's hard to believe it's possible, but we can forget *that* God saved us and *how* he saved us. We forget we didn't deserve saving. We forget we were saved by God. We forget the suffering required to save us. We forget to worship God for saving us.

*What's the antidote for such serious spiritual amnesia?* Let's see how God cures the Israelites' amnesia in Exodus 12 so that we can improve our spiritual memories too.

### Salvation Is by Grace Alone 12:1–6

Israel could not save themselves; God had to do it. God initiated salvation (12:1–2), designed salvation (12:3–5), and provided salvation (12:6). He reset their calendar so that the beginning of the year reminded them of the beginning of their salvation. His salvation blueprint was titled "Substitution," saving Israel from death by a lamb dying in their place.

*Grace + something = nothing.*
*Grace + zero = everything.*

*"So God starts salvation. I guess I have to complete it, then?"*
*Nope, you just receive it.*

## Salvation Is by Faith Alone 12:7–11

Israel needed faith to receive God's salvation. They needed faith to kill the lamb, faith to sprinkle its blood around their front doors, faith to burn the lamb, faith to eat the lamb, and faith to pack up and prepare to leave Egypt. They needed faith to believe "it is the LORD's Passover" (12:11).

***For salvation to be by grace alone,***
***it must be received by faith alone.***

*"So we're to put our faith in the blood of the lamb.*
*Then do we do our part?" Nope.*

## Salvation Is by Blood Alone 12:12–13

God taught the Israelites there could be no salvation without suffering, blood, and death. "For I will pass through the land of Egypt that night, and I will strike all the firstborn in the land of Egypt, both man and beast; and on all the gods of Egypt I will execute judgments: I am the LORD. The blood shall be a sign for you, on the houses where you are. And when I see the blood, I will pass over you, and no plague will befall you to destroy you, when I strike the land of Egypt" (12:12–13).

***The Lord judges the bloodless***
***but passes over the blood-covered.***

*"So we don't have any part.*
*What does that mean for us?"*
*It means worship.*

## Salvation Is for the Glory of God Alone 12:14

Why does God save in this way? So that he gets all the glory. "This day shall be for you a memorial day, and you shall keep it as a feast to the LORD; throughout your generations, as a statute forever, you shall keep it as a feast" (12:14). He instituted a memorial to remind Israel of his salvation and give an opportunity to celebrate his salvation. When Moses told Israel about this salvation, the people bowed their heads and worshiped (12:27). That's exactly where God wants us.

*Plan to remember your salvation,*
*or you can plan on forgetting it.*

### Changing Our Story with God's Story

God has given us an even greater salvation to remember and celebrate in the New Testament. In Jesus, we see even more clearly that salvation is by grace alone, by faith alone, by blood alone, and for the glory of God alone. In the Lord's Supper, God has given us an unforgettable reminder of Jesus and his salvation. Let's bow our heads and celebrate Jesus.

**Summary:** What's the antidote for spiritual amnesia? *Use the Lord's Supper as a reminder to celebrate God's sovereign salvation forever.*

**Question:** What's your plan for remembering your salvation on a daily and weekly basis?

**Prayer:** My Great Savior, I confess that I forget your unforgettable salvation. Improve my memory so that I can improve my praise.

**Remember God's strong hand, and you'll forget your weak hands.**

Hear God's Story | Change Your Story | Tell the Story | Change Others' Stories

15

# God's Hand and Our Hands

EXODUS 13:1–10

Without reminders we'd never remember. One of the greatest benefits of digital devices is that we can set reminders for everything. In the pre-smartphone era, which seems like a million years ago, it was easier to forget appointments and events. They were written in our diaries, but they didn't jump out of our pockets to remind us just before the due time. Now we can set beeping and buzzing reminders for everything.

What about spiritual reminders? *What spiritual alarms does God give us to remind us of special events and appointments?*

In the previous chapter, God instituted the annual Passover to remind the Israelites of God's hand in their salvation. In Exodus 13:1–10, God instituted the Feast of Unleavened Bread to remind the Israelites of what their hands were to do in their sanctification. Let's hear these annual alarms to remind us of what we must remember about God.

## God's Hand Separates from Slavery 13:3, 9

"Moses said to the people, 'Remember this day in which you came out from Egypt, out of the house of slavery, for by a strong hand the Lord brought you out from this place'" (13:3). God's strong saving hand is also spotlighted in verse 9. God is saying

"Remember, remember. Remember my strong hand, remember my saving hand."

***Remember God's strong hand,***
***and you'll forget your weak hands.***

*"If that's what God's hand did,*
*what are our hands to do?"*
*Separate from sin.*

## Our Hands Are to Separate from Sin 13:3–8

Moses declared, "By a strong hand the Lord brought you out from this place. No leavened bread shall be eaten. . . . Seven days you shall eat unleavened bread, and on the seventh day there shall be a feast to the Lord" (13:3, 6). To prepare for this week, they were to purge their houses and property of all yeast. "No leavened bread shall be seen with you, and no leaven shall be seen with you in all your territory" (13:7). Their hands were to throw away all yeast and then not touch any for seven days.

Why all this concern about tiny pieces of yeast? Moses explains, "And it shall be to you as a sign on your hand and as a memorial between your eyes, that the law of the Lord may be in your mouth. For with a strong hand the Lord has brought you out of Egypt" (13:9). No yeast in your mouth so that God's law will be in your mouth. Moses was using yeast as a picture of sin. God's hand saved you from sin, therefore use your hands to sanctify you from sin.

***If we remember God's hand,***
***we'll get more than just holy hands.***

### Changing Our Story with God's Story

The apostle Paul translates this into New Testament language for us when preparing the Corinthians for the New Testament observance of the Lord's Supper. "Your boasting is not good. Do you not know that a little leaven leavens the whole lump? Cleanse out the old leaven that you may be a new lump, as you really are unleavened. For Christ, our Passover lamb, has been sacrificed. Let us therefore celebrate the festival, not with the old leaven, the leaven of malice and evil, but with the unleavened bread of sincerity and truth" (1 Cor. 5:6–8). Remember Christ's saving hand so that you will have sanctifying hands. Remember, a little sin spreads faster and farther than a little yeast.

**Summary:** What spiritual alarms does God give us to remind us of special events and appointments? *Use the Lord's Supper to remember Christ's saving hand to motivate and move your holy hands.*

**Question:** What "little" sin is spreading and needs to be removed from your life?

**Prayer:** Deliverer, use the Lord's Supper to remind me of your mighty hands of salvation and to give me mighty hands of sanctification.

**God judged his firstborn Son to save all his sons and daughters.**

16

# Extreme Salvation for Extreme Sinners

## EXODUS 13:11–16

Melody and Bob hadn't been married for long when a spiritual problem arose. Melody was an optimist and loved to hear their pastor's sermons about Christ's love in saving sinners. She tended to minimize sin. Bob was more of a pessimist and felt that his pastor didn't stress God's judgment enough. Bob tended to minimize salvation.

When they went to talk to their pastor about it, he helped them to see that both emphases were in the Bible, and both were needed. He first took them to the New Testament and showed how, at the cross, we see both judgment of sin and salvation from sin. The New Testament maximizes sin and maximizes salvation. He then took them to the Old Testament, to Exodus 13:11–16, and demonstrated how the Old Testament also maximized sin and maximized salvation.

Most of us tend to fall into either the Melody or the Bob extreme. Sometimes we can swing between the two extremes. *How do we avoid unbiblical extremes and find biblical balance?*

### God Saves through Judgment 13:14–15

When the Israelites came into the promised land, they were to "set apart to the Lord all that first opens the womb. All the firstborn of your animals that are males shall be the Lord's" (13:12).

When future Israelites asked why they sacrificed the firstborn to the Lord, they were to be told the exodus story. In summary, God saved Israel out of Egypt by judging the firstborn of Egypt, therefore the firstborn in Israel were to be sacrificed to the Lord as a reminder that God saves through judging sin (13:14–15).

***God judges sin so that he can save from sin.***

*"Everyone was sinful, so why didn't God judge everyone?"*
*Because the Israelites trusted in a substitute to die in their place.*

## God Saves through Substitution 13:15

God saved through substitution at the first Passover. Then in the annual celebrations of the Passover, they were reminded of this substitution again.

In the firstborn-to-God rule, God instituted a way that Israel would be reminded of substitution more frequently. Every time a male firstborn came into the world, it/he was to be offered to God as a substitute for every other animal. The firstborn was sacrificed to God so that the rest of the born would live.

The only exceptions to this firstborn-to-the-Lord rule were firstborn donkeys and firstborn sons. Firstborn donkeys could be redeemed and replaced with a lamb and firstborn sons with money (13:13; Num. 18:16). Instead of offering a donkey, they could offer a lamb. Instead of offering a son, they could offer money.

Why donkeys? Most likely it was the practical reason that they functioned as the pickup trucks of their day and therefore God allowed an alternative sacrifice. But whether the firstborn was sacrificed or redeemed, the whole idea of substitution, something in place of something, was prominent.

***God judged his firstborn Son to save all his sons and daughters.***

## Changing Our Story with God's Story

What does this maximizing of both sin and salvation do? It helps us never to minimize our sin or our Savior. Jesus was fully judged so that we could be fully saved. A full judgment and a full salvation help us to walk the gospel tightrope with one side of the balancing pole labeled "biblical pessimism" and the other side "biblical optimism." Balance does not come from abandoning both but by holding both at the same time.

**Summary:** How do we avoid unbiblical extremes and find the biblical balance? *Find biblical balance by remembering that God saved you from sin by judging the Savior in your place.*

**Question:** Are you tempted to maximize sin or maximize salvation? Why is that and how can you correct it?

**Prayer:** My Savior, thank you for saving me in a way that maximizes my sin and maximizes my salvation. Help me to hold both extremes at the same time so that I can maintain a safe and saving biblical balance.

**When we can't save ourselves, we can then be saved by God.**

Hear God's Story | Change Your Story | Tell the Story | Change Others' Stories

17

# God's Surprising Solution to Our Greatest Problem

EXODUS 14

Our greatest problem is that we cannot save ourselves. I remember many times in my teens and early twenties trying to do so. I turned over so many new leaves that I deforested the Amazon. I tried so hard, then I gave up, then I blamed God, then I tried harder, then I gave up, then I blamed God, and on and on it went.

Perhaps you're in the same desperate dilemma (or you know someone who is). Wanting to change but unable to change. Wanting to be saved but unable to save yourself. *What must I do to be saved?* Thankfully, in my early twenties, I found an amazing answer to this desperate dilemma, and I want to share it with you. It's in Exodus 14.

## Salvation Is Not from Us 14:1–12

God had delivered Israel from Egypt but now seemed to have led them into a dead end that would end in their death. The Egyptians regretted their decision to let Israel go and set out to pursue them (14:1–9). As the Egyptians closed in on them, the Israelites realized that they were trapped with the sea in front of them, mountains on one side, desert on the other, and the enemy closing fast. They were cornered, defenseless, helpless, terrified, and despairing. Realizing there was nothing they could do to save themselves, they turned on Moses and God (14:10–12). Why did God let this happen? To teach Israel the most important spiritual lesson.

***When we can't save ourselves,***
***we can then be saved by God.***

*"How did Israel learn this?"*
*Let's hear God's message through Moses.*

## Salvation Is of the Lord 14:13–31

What was Moses's message to helpless Israel? "Fear not, stand firm, and see the salvation of the Lord, which he will work for you today. For the Egyptians whom you see today, you shall never see again. The Lord will fight for you, and you have only to be silent" (14:13–14). Don't move your hands, your feet, your tongue, or even your brain. Be still, be silent, and watch God do what you cannot do.

God parted the Red Sea, Israel went through perfectly dry, Egypt tried to follow, and the Egyptians were all swept away by the returning water. God was glorified in saving Israel and in defeating Egypt (14:15–31). "Thus the Lord saved Israel that day from the hand of the Egyptians, and Israel saw the Egyptians dead on the seashore. Israel saw the great power that the Lord used against the Egyptians, so the people feared the Lord, and they believed in the Lord and in his servant Moses" (14:30–31).

***When we can do nothing for God,***
***God can do everything for us.***

### Changing Our Story with God's Story

What a surprising solution and amazing answer to our desperate dilemma! This solution and answer is given to us even more clearly in the New Testament. At the cross we stand perfectly still and see God perfectly glorified in the salvation of his people and in the defeat of all his enemies. We don't move an atom. As Paul put it, "For by grace you have been saved through faith. And this is not your own doing; it is the gift of God, not a result of works, so that no one may boast" (Eph. 2:8–9). What a beautiful surprise!

**Summary:** What must I do to be saved? *Stop, stand still, and see the salvation of the Lord.* Even those of us who've already been saved can still stop again, stand still again, and see the salvation of the Lord again and again.

**Question:** How can you remind yourself every day that salvation is 100 percent of the Lord? What difference would that make to your life and witness?

**Prayer:** Great and Gracious Savior, thank you for your 100 percent salvation which I 100 percent trust. Help me to be 100 percent surprised and give 100 percent to tell 100 percent of people about your 100 percent salvation.

## Increase your feelings in song by increasing theology in your songs.

18

# What Songs Should We Sing?

EXODUS 15:1–21

How do we decide what songs to sing in worship? That question has divided many churches. Some songs focus only on positives. Others focus primarily on our feelings. And some focus primarily on Christian life. Such imbalanced diets will unbalance our souls and our spiritual lives.

*How do we decide what to sing?* Moses's song in Exodus 15 gives us three biblical criteria for worship songs.

## Sing Songs That Praise God's Judgments 15:3–10

After God had delivered the Israelites through the Red Sea and destroyed the Egyptians in the Red Sea, Moses stirred up himself and the Israelites to sing praise to God.

> I will sing to the Lord, for he has triumphed gloriously;
> the horse and his rider he has thrown into the sea.
> The Lord is my strength and my song,
> and he has become my salvation;
> this is my God, and I will praise him. (15:1–2)

What does Moses sing about first? He sings about God's judgments. He praises him for his just judgments (15:3–5), his awesome judgments (15:6–8), his easy judgments (15:9–10a), and his irreversible judgments (15:10b).

*God's judgments are for commendation not condemnation.*

*"Isn't that too negative?"*
*This is just the starting point.*

## Sing Songs That Praise God's Character 15:11–12

Moses next praises the character of God.

> Who is like you, O LORD, among the gods?
> Who is like you, majestic in holiness,
> awesome in glorious deeds, doing wonders?
> You stretched out your right hand;
> the earth swallowed them. (15:11–12)

God is incomparably majestic, holy, awesome, glorious, and wonderful.

***Increase your feelings in song by increasing theology in your songs.***

*"We're to sing about judgment and*
*theology; I get that. What about salvation?"*
*Moses climaxes with that theme.*

## Sing Songs That Praise God's Salvation 15:13–21

Having praised God's judgments and character, Moses turns to God's salvation. God lovingly redeems his people (15:13a), guides his people (15:13b), protects his people (15:14–16), and communes with his people (15:17–18).

Listen to some of these beautiful words with New Testament ears:

> You have led in your steadfast love the people whom you have redeemed;
> you have guided them by your strength to your holy abode. . . .
> You will bring them in and plant them on your own mountain,
> the place, O LORD, which you have made for your abode,
> the sanctuary, O LORD, which your hands have established.
> The LORD will reign forever and ever." (15:13–18)

Salvation lyrics are brighter when sung against the dark background of judgment and louder when built on the strong foundation of God's character.

*This is my story, this is my song,*
*praising my Savior all the day long.*[1]

## Changing Our Story with God's Story

Moses has given us three clear criteria to guide us in how to express our love to God in song. It's a beautiful balance of God's judgment, God's character, and God's salvation, with each amplifying the other. The Psalms further support and demonstrate these criteria. The best songs in Christian history have also been guided by these criteria, right up to the present day. Look at the lyrics of songs like "In Christ Alone" and "Jesus, Strong and Kind."

**Summary:** How do we decide what to sing? *Sing balanced, God-centered, God-exalting songs to please God and do good to our souls.*

**Question:** What will be the effect upon us and others if we sing such songs?

**Prayer:** Praiseworthy God, I praise you for your judgments, your character, and your salvation. Help me to sing the best songs ever in the best way ever to the best God ever.

1 Fanny Crosby, "Blessed Assurance," 1873.

**God heals greater spiritual sickness by sending lesser physical sickness.**

19

# The God Who Heals

EXODUS 15:22–27

My eighty-one-year-old dad died in the past year. He had suffered a number of strokes over the years and deteriorated rapidly in the last few weeks. I'm only in my fifties, but I've already had a number of illnesses. Sickness, disease, and death cast a long shadow over our lives. *How can we brighten the shadowy valley of sickness?* God teaches us about his sovereignty over sickness in Exodus 15:22–27.

## God Heals by Preventing Sickness 15:26

After three days without water in the wilderness, the Israelites eventually found some at Marah. However, when they drank it, it was bitter, and they started complaining. Moses prayed to the Lord, and God told Moses to throw a log into the water, sweetening it and making it drinkable (15:22–25).

Using this as a teachable moment, God draws out a principle for Israel from this test: "If you will diligently listen to the voice of the Lord your God, and do that which is right in his eyes, and give ear to his commandments and keep all his statutes, I will put none of the diseases on you that I put on the Egyptians, for I am the Lord, your healer" (15:26).

God teaches them that he is in control of sickness and disease and that he can demonstrate this by punishing our sin with sickness and by preventing sickness with our holiness. In this sense God can say, "I am the Lord, your healer."

***Prevention is better than cure, but both are in God's hands.***

*"Does that mean that all sickness is a punishment for sin?"*
*No, God also uses sickness to test us.*

## God Heals by Testing with Sickness 15:23–24

"There he tested them" (15:25). God sets tests to help his people learn. Just as God turned the bitter waters into sweet waters, God can turn our bitter experiences into sweet experiences by using them to educate us. In this sense also God can say, "I am the Lord, your healer."

***God heals greater spiritual sickness by sending lesser physical sickness.***

*"So God can prevent sickness and improve us with sickness,*
*but how about removing it?"*
*Watch this.*

## God Heals by Removing Sickness 15:25–26

God can and may remove sickness at times, and he did that at Marah. He healed the water and the people's sickness. In this sense God can say, "I am the Lord, your healer."

God does not heal all sickness on this earth. But, for his people, he will heal all sickness eventually and eternally. When his people die, he cures them of all soul-sickness. When their bodies are resurrected and reunited with their souls, he forever heals them of all bodily sickness too. In this fullest sense, God can say, "I am the Lord, your healer." Israel got a foretaste, a sip of that, at the end of Exodus 15: "Then they came to Elim, where there were twelve springs of water and seventy palm trees, and they encamped there by the water" (15:27).

***Our complete healing comes with God's complete salvation.***

## Changing Our Story with God's Story

We love the Old Testament healings of the Lord our healer. But we love the New Testament healings even more. There we see Jesus healing multiple sick people of multiple diseases and sicknesses.

He also heals the bitterest and most painful disease of all, the disease of sin. "And when Jesus heard it, he said to them, 'Those who are well have no need of a physician, but those who are sick. I came not to call the righteous, but sinners'" (Mark 2:17). We are able to drink the sweet water of salvation because he tasted the bitter dregs of sin's judgment. With his wounds we are healed (Isa. 53:5).

**Summary:** How can we brighten the shadowy valley of sickness? *Remember, God can prevent, use, and heal sickness, especially the sickness of sin.*

**Question:** How many diseases and sins has God prevented, used, and healed in your life?

**Prayer:** Lord My Healer, heal me by preventing, using, and curing sin and sickness for my good and your glory.

# We deserve heavenly fire, but God sends heavenly food.

20

# Complainers or Praisers?

## EXODUS 16:1–12

Whiners are not winners. When we complain about our circumstances to others, we're effectively (though usually unintentionally) accusing God and slandering his character. We're saying God doesn't care, God doesn't know what he's doing, and God can't do anything about this.

This is not a winning strategy. These are horrendous and dangerous slanders against God. *How do I move from complaining to praising?* Exodus 16:1–12 moves us by demonstrating how complaints are a heart problem not a God problem.

### God Provides for Complainers 16:1–4, 6–8

Forty-five days after leaving Egypt the Israelites entered the wilderness and started their journey to the promised land (16:1). They'd hardly started, though, when the people complained about Moses's leadership and their hunger (16:2–3). Moses warned them that they were actually complaining about God not him (16:7–8).

If I'd just delivered the Israelites from Egyptian slavery, Egyptian soldiers, and the Red Sea, I think I'd rain fire from heaven upon them for such ingratitude. But instead God rained bread from heaven upon them and promised to keep doing so (16:4, 6–8).

*We deserve heavenly fire, but God sends heavenly food.*

*"God does care and he does provide, but why did he let this situation develop in the first place?"*
*To test his people.*

## God Tests Complainers 16:4–5

God didn't let the moment pass without teaching the Israelites how to trust and obey him. Instead of giving them enough bread for days, he promised enough supply for each day and told them to take just enough for each day (16:4). He gave them double on the sixth day and told them not to look for it on the seventh day (16:5). God explains why he did it this way: "That I may test them, whether they will walk in my law or not" (16:4).

***When we're complaining, God is testing.***

*"So God does know what he's doing.*
*But what's his aim in the provision and the test?"*
*To reveal himself.*

## God Reveals Himself to Complainers 16:9–12

If I were leading this bunch of ungrateful moaners and whiners, I'd leave them right there in the wilderness. Instead, God met them right there in the wilderness, so that they would see not just the glorious provision of bread but the glorious God behind it. "They looked toward the wilderness, and behold, the glory of the Lord appeared in the cloud" (16:10). God had a greater design in the provision of bread and the revealing of his glory: "You shall know that I am the Lord your God" (16:12). He wanted them to know him and have a relationship with him.

***God doesn't run and hide from us but runs to us and reveals himself to us.***

## Changing Our Story with God's Story

Fast-forward two thousand years, and we find the same nation hungry and complaining in the desert (John 6:7–9). In Jesus, God ran to them, provided for them, and showed them so much of his glory that the people thought he was the second Moses and exclaimed, "This is indeed the Prophet who is to come into the world!" (John 6:14). Jesus revealed even more of his glory to the disciples when he later said, "I am the bread of life; whoever comes to me shall not hunger" (John 6:35).

Fast-forward another two thousand years to us, and we find that God's people still haven't changed too much. We're just the same as Israel of two thousand and four thousand years ago. But thankfully God is the same too.

**Summary:** How do I move from complaining to praising? *Turn your complaint into a chorus by seeing that God is providing for you, testing you, and revealing his glory to you.*

**Question:** How has God turned your complaints into praises?

**Prayer:** Glorious God, I'm ashamed to admit that I'm too often a complainer and too rarely a praiser. Use this passage to turn my complaints into praises for your glory and my good.

**When God calls us to trust harder, why do we decide to try harder?**

Hear God's Story | Change Your Story | Tell the Story | Change Others' Stories

21

# The Secret to Exam Success

## EXODUS 16:13–36

When I was in high school, the only time I did any work was when my teacher scheduled an exam. If I knew material wasn't going to be tested, I never bothered to learn it. If it was tested, I had to learn it.

Regrettably, many of us bring the same minimalist spirit into our Christian lives. Unless we are tested, we don't learn. If we are tested, we have to learn. That was also true of the Israelites, which explains why in Exodus 16:13–36 God gave Israel three tests that he still gives today. *Why does God test us?* Here are three reasons from this passage.

### God Tests Our Trust in Him 16:13–21

Despite Israel's complaining, God provided both bread and quail for them. The bread was called manna, and it came with the condition that they gather only as much as they needed each day and leave nothing for the next day. This was to test whether Israel really trusted God to provide every day for their needs.

Of course, some distrusted God and attempted to keep some overnight. The result? "It bred worms and stank. And Moses was angry with them" (16:20).

*When God calls us to trust harder,*
*why do we decide to try harder?*

*"Israel failed that test. Does God give them another chance?"*
*Yes, he tests their rest in him.*

## God Tests Our Rest in Him 16:22–30

The next test was whether Israel would rest in God. Although allowed to gather only one day's supply at a time, on the sixth day they were allowed to gather twice as much so that they would rest in God on the Sabbath day (16:22–26). God promised that in these circumstances the bread would not rot on the second day, and it didn't.

But yes, you've guessed it, some decided to go out on the seventh day anyway to gather more, and they found none (16:27). This time the Lord was angry that they failed the test of rest (16:28–30).

***When God promises rest, why do we choose restlessness?***

*"A second fail. Surely God doesn't give them a third chance."*
*Yes, he does. He tests their memory of him.*

## God Tests Our Memory of Him 16:31–36

Knowing Israel's tendency toward spiritual amnesia, God tests whether Israel will remember his provision. "Moses said to Aaron, 'Take a jar, and put an omer of manna in it, and place it before the LORD to be kept throughout your generations'" (16:33).

We're not told the final result of this third test. We're told they ate the manna for forty years, but not whether they remembered it longer than that. We're left hanging, asking, "Will Israel pass the test of remembering this provision at the end of a forty-year lesson?" So far they've only taught us how to fail.

***When God teaches the same lesson for forty years,***
***how can we forget the lesson in forty seconds?***

## Changing Our Story with God's Story

When I taught seminary students, I often heard them complaining about professors giving them "busy work." They were tested just to be tested, rather than tested to help them learn. God never does that. When he tests our trust, our rest, and our memory, it's always necessary, always constructive, always helpful. In some ways the whole Christian life is a lifelong test of our trust in Christ, our rest in Christ, and our memory of Christ. But here's the encouraging secret: Christ is with us in the tests, wants us to pass the tests, and helps us to pass the tests.

**Summary:** Why does God test us? *Whatever situation you are facing, pass God's tests by relying on, resting in, and remembering Jesus.*

**Question:** In your current tests, what grade would God give you for relying upon, resting in, and remembering Jesus?

**Prayer:** Wise Tester, I confess I often fail your tests by relying on myself, running around in circles, and forgetting Jesus. Please forgive me and teach me how to rely on, rest in, and remember Jesus.

God is not to be tested but trusted.

Hear God's Story | Change Your Story | Tell the Story | Change Others' Stories

22

# God Takes an Exam

## EXODUS 17:1–7

Imagine you're a teacher, a really good teacher. You give a simple short exam of three questions. The whole class fails badly. The next day, the students come to you. You're expecting them to say, "We're really sorry. We're terrible students, but we're going to learn and study much better in the future."

Instead they say, "Teacher, sit down and take this exam we've put together for you and let's see how you do."

How would you feel? What would you say or do? I think I'd throw their exam in the trash can and throw them out of the classroom. The cheek!

Yet that's what Israel did to God in Exodus 17:1–7. In the previous chapter, God tested Israel with three questions: Will you trust me? Will you rest in me? Will you remember me? They failed badly.

In this chapter, believe it or not, Israel turns the tables and tests God with two questions: Will you provide for us? Are you present with us? What daring and dangerous questions. How will God react to such an impudent challenge? *Should we ever test God?* Let's see what happened in this case.

### We Sometimes Test God 17:1–4, 7

After some days walking in the wilderness, the Israelites "camped at Rephidim, but there was no water for the people to drink. Therefore the people quarreled with Moses and said, 'Give us water to drink.'

And Moses said to them, 'Why do you quarrel with me? Why do you test the LORD?'" (17:1–2).

Indeed, they argued so violently with Moses that he cried to the Lord, "What shall I do with this people? They are almost ready to stone me" (17:4). No wonder, later in the passage, we're told that "he called the name of the place Massah [testing] and Meribah [quarreling], because of the quarreling of the people of Israel, and because they tested the LORD by saying, 'Is the LORD among us or not?'" (17:7).

Israel tested God's provision (Will you give us water?) and God's presence (Are you among us or not?).

***God is not to be tested but trusted.***

*"So what's the result if we dare to test God?"*
*God has never failed an exam.*

## God Always Passes the Test 17:5–6

What would you do in these circumstances? Remember God had recently delivered the Israelites from Egyptian slavery, Egyptian soldiers, and the Red Sea. He'd also provided bread and quail from heaven. And yet Israel questions his provision and his presence. How would you respond? I think I'd say, "I'm not answering your silly questions."

But God didn't. He submitted himself to the test and answered their questions by providing water from a rock and standing with Moses as he did so. God said, "'Behold, I will stand before you there on the rock at Horeb, and you shall strike the rock, and water shall come out of it, and the people will drink.' And Moses did so, in the sight of the elders of Israel" (17:6).

God answered the questions about his provision and his presence: I always provide and I'm always present.

***God can answer every question,***
***but we shouldn't ask every question.***

## Changing Our Story with God's Story

We still test God today, don't we? It looks different—we're surrounded by cars and digital devices instead of camels and desert sand. But we still question God's provision and presence. As we look back on our wilderness walk, we see many places named Massah and Meribah, many places we tested God and argued with God. Did God ever fail the test? No, he took the same test again and again and always scored 100 percent. He even came to this earth and submitted to testing in the wilderness before prohibiting the devil from testing him any further (Matt. 4:7).

**Summary:** Should we ever test God? *Instead of testing God, trust God for his provision and presence in times of testing.*

**Question:** In what way is God testing you? In what way are you testing God?

**Prayer:** You, Lord, are present and providing in my life. You have passed these tests many times. Help me therefore to stop testing you and start trusting you.

**When we put faith before family, God will put faith in our families.**

Hear God's Story | Change Your Story | Tell the Story | Change Others' Stories

23

# Faith and Family

EXODUS 18:1–12

Faith and family can conflict. When they do, some people sacrifice faith for family. Other people sacrifice family for faith. *How should we connect and relate faith and family?* Let's look at the connection between both in Moses's life in Exodus 18:1–12.

## Faith Comes before Family 18:1–4

Moses's life was a testimony to faith being more important than family. Three times faith resulted in him being separated from his family. The first was when his parents by faith put him in a basket on the Nile River, trusting God to look after him (Heb. 11:23). Though Moses was separated from his Israelite family, God brought him into Pharoah's family.

The second separation came when he chose to suffer affliction with the Israelites rather than enjoy all the privileges and pleasures of being an Egyptian royal (Heb. 11:24–27). When Moses separated from his Egyptian family, God brought him into a Midianite family.

The third separation was God's call to leave his Midianite family and go to Egypt to deliver God's family. Three experiences of separation from family but also three acts of faith in God.

***God gives us families to bring us to faith,***
***but families must never keep us from faith.***

*"I get that faith comes before family,*
*but does that mean I just forget family?"*
*No, faith first does not mean family last.*

## Faith Remembers Family 18:5–7

When Moses's father-in-law heard of all that God had done for Moses and Israel in the exodus, he gathered Moses's family and set off to meet him in the wilderness. When Moses received word of this, "Moses went out to meet his father-in-law and bowed down and kissed him. And they asked each other of their welfare and went into the tent" (18:7). Although Moses put his faith before his family, he did not forget his family. When opportunity arose, he gladly and lovingly reunited with them.

***Faith puts family second, but never last.***

*"So how did they catch up when they reunited?"*
*They talked about God and his acts.*

## Faith Unites Family 18:8–12

Let's listen in on their family reunion.

> Then Moses told his father-in-law all that the LORD had done to Pharaoh and to the Egyptians for Israel's sake, all the hardship that had come upon them in the way, and how the LORD had delivered them. And Jethro rejoiced for all the good that the LORD had done to Israel, in that he had delivered them out of the hand of the Egyptians.
>
> Jethro said, "Blessed be the LORD, who has delivered you out of the hand of the Egyptians and out of the hand of Pharaoh and has delivered the people from under the hand of the Egyptians. Now I know that the LORD is greater than all gods, because in this affair they dealt arrogantly with the people." And Jethro, Moses' father-in-law, brought a burnt offering and sacrifices to God; and Aaron came with all the elders of Israel to eat bread with Moses' father-in-law before God. (18:8–12)

Jethro listened to Moses (18:8), rejoiced with Moses (18:9), confessed to Moses (18:10–11), sacrificed with Moses (18:12a), and fellowshiped with Moses (18:12b). Faith may separate for a time but ultimately it unites family closer than ever before.

*When we put faith before family,*
*God will put faith in our families.*

### Changing Our Story with God's Story

Moses's willingness to give up everything for God reminds us of Christ's willingness to give up his heavenly family for the sake of his earthly family. Just as Moses gave up his earthly comforts to serve God and his people, Christ gave up all heavenly comforts to do the same. Christ put faith before family, for the sake of his family's faith, and ultimately expanded and united his family in faith.

**Summary:** How should we connect and relate faith and family? *Connect faith and family so that our family comes to faith.*

**Question:** How would you describe the relationship between your faith and your family?

**Prayer:** God of Families, thank you for godly families and that through them you are building the kingdom of God. Build my family so that we can build your family too.

**No amount of human law can subdue human lawlessness.**

24

# The Blessing of Law and Order

EXODUS 18:13–27

Even at the best of times, this world is chaotic and disordered. We crave harmony and peace, but it's so rare and so brief. That's why a functioning legal system is such a blessing from God. It's one of the ways in which he defeats chaos and disorder and creates harmony and peace in our world and lives.

*How can we join with God in this great work of restoring law and order in our lives and in the lives of those around us?* Exodus 18:13–27 narrates how God did this with the Israelites.

## We Produce Lawlessness and Disorder 18:13–18

When the Israelites came out of Egypt, they were united and orderly (Ex. 13:18). Given all they'd been through and all that God had done for them, we might have expected this to last. It didn't. Soon there was chaos, disorder, fighting, and arguing among the people.

Before long, Moses was spending all day every day judging all the disputes of Israel (18:13–14). Jethro, his father-in-law, was watching this and basically said, "What do you think you're doing?" Moses replied, "The people come to me to inquire of God; when they have a dispute, they come to me and I decide between one person and another, and I make them know the statutes of God and his laws" (18:15–16).

Jethro appreciated Moses's efforts but told him he was attempting the impossible. "What you're doing is not good. You and the people with you will certainly wear yourselves out, for the thing is too heavy for you. You are not able to do it alone" (18:17–18). There was way too much lawlessness for one man to deal with.

***No amount of human law can subdue human lawlessness.***

*"Is there any hope of law and order in this world?"*
*Yes, from outside of this world.*

## God Provides Law and Order 18:19–27

God used Jethro to reform the justice system in three ways. First, he instructed Moses to seek the help of God by bringing the cases to God. "You shall represent the people before God and bring their cases to God" (18:19).

Second, Moses was to proactively teach the people about God's law and what it meant for their lives. "You shall warn them about the statutes and the laws, and make them know the way in which they must walk and what they must do" (18:20).

Third, Moses was to delegate easier cases to other just men to judge (18:21–22). "If you do this," Jethro assured him, "God will direct you, you will be able to endure, and all this people also will go to their place in peace" (18:23).

***God restores harmony and peace***
***by reinforcing law and order.***

## Changing Our Story with God's Story

God worked through Jethro to replace chaos and order with harmony and peace. He did that through the blessing of more law and more lawgivers.

In the New Testament, God worked through Jesus to replace chaos and disorder with harmony and peace. He did this at the cross by punishing the lawgiver in place of lawbreakers like us. The cross was the only place of perfect justice the world has ever seen. Though it looked like chaos and disorder, God was making harmony and peace through it all.

**Summary:** How can we join with God in the great work of restoring law and order in our lives and in the lives of those around us? *Join with God in his restorative work by proclaiming the great law-keeping, law-upholding, law-satisfying, and law-liberating work of Christ on the cross.*

**Question:** What will you do today to bring harmony and peace out of chaos and disorder?

**Prayer:** Lawgiver, thank you for your perfect laws that help this imperfect world to function. Thank you also for Jesus Christ who kept the law perfectly, suffered its penalties perfectly, and will one day rule with it perfectly.

**We sell ourselves to sin for nothing, but God buys us back from sin with everything.**

25

# The Four *R*'s

## EXODUS 19:1–6

What's the greatest problem in the world? Disease? Racism? Riots? Recession? These are all big problems but not one of them is the greatest problem. As we see in the Bible again and again, the greatest problem is attempting self-salvation. The core idea is that we can be saved by our works, our obedience, our commandment-keeping. We can offer God enough law-keeping to persuade him to save us.

Why is that the greatest problem? Because no matter how hard we try, we cannot save ourselves or please God. Any attempt to do so ultimately downgrades God's law. We know that in our consciences, don't we? We're not happy, God's not happy, and the law's not happy.

*So how do we solve the world's greatest problem?* God solves it in Exodus 19:1–6, when he officially constituted Israel as his nation. He solves it with four *R*'s.

### God Redeems Us 19:3–4

Three months after God brought the Israelites out of Egypt, they arrived at Mount Sinai, just as God had promised Moses in Exodus 3:12. God called Moses up the mountain and said to him: "Thus you shall say to the house of Jacob, and tell the people of Israel: 'You yourselves have seen what I did to the Egyptians, and how I bore you on eagles' wings'" (19:3–4). In a short sentence, God sums up his redemption: I destroyed your enemies and I carried you like a mother bird might carry her young.

***We sell ourselves to sin for nothing,***
***but God buys us back from sin with everything.***

*"What does he redeem us to?"*
*To relationship with him.*

## God Relates to Us 19:4

This redemption was not just an act of great power but also an act of great love. "I brought you to myself" (19:4). He brought them out of Egyptian hate and into his loving embrace. He didn't just bring them to a mountain; he brought them to himself.

***We run from God but God runs to us.***

*"How does he keep our relationship with him healthy and happy?"*
*With relational rules.*

## God Regulates Us 19:5

"Now therefore, if you will indeed obey my voice and keep my covenant . . ." (19:5). Here's the third *R*. There's nothing more important than keeping the third *R* third. God's not saying, "If you keep my rules, I'll redeem you and be in relationship with you." No, he's saying, "I've redeemed you and brought you into a covenant relationship; therefore, in light of all I've done for you and as an expression of covenant gratitude to me, keep my relational rules. I've established my covenant with you. Now, keep it healthy and happy by keeping my covenant rules."

***We obey to worship our Savior, not to earn salvation.***

*"How does God encourage us here?"*
*With a great reward.*

## God Rewards Us 19:5–6

To further encourage obedience, God promises them a triple reward: "You shall be my treasured possession among all peoples, for all the earth is mine; and you shall be to me a kingdom of priests and a holy nation" (19:5–6). God promises a special depth and intimacy in Israel's relationship with him.

*Reward is not the basis of salvation.*
*It is the bonus in salvation.*

### Changing Our Story with God's Story

Our greatest problem is self-salvation or rule-redemption. God's solution is redemption > relationship > rules > reward (see also John 14:15–21). God redeems us for relationship, provides rules to keep that relationship happy and healthy, and rewards covenantal obedience as a bonus.

**Summary:** How do we solve the greatest problem in the world? God solves it, and we respond *by obeying God's rules out of loving gratitude for his covenant redemption.*

**Question:** How do you keep the four *R*'s in the right order?

**Prayer:** Redeemer, thank you for bringing me into a relationship with you. Help me to obey your rules to keep our relationship healthy and happy.

God longs for us, more than for our obedience.

Hear God's Story | Change Your Story | Tell the Story | Change Others' Stories

26

# The Love of God in the Law of God

EXODUS 20

How do you view the law of God? Maybe, like many, you view it as a threat. "It's a threat to my salvation and to my happiness. Give me God's love over God's law any day."

But what if I told you there's another way of looking at God's law? That we can see the love of God in the law of God? You don't want to miss out on God's love, do you? *How can we experience God's love in God's law?* Come with me to Exodus 20, where we'll discover four ways to experience God's love in God's law.

## God's Love Liberates Us 20:1–2

God's law starts with God's salvation, not our obedience. "I am the Lord your God, who brought you out of the land of Egypt, out of the house of slavery" (20:2). That's God's saving love, and it comes before one law is even announced. God's love is the foundation of God's law. Therefore, let's love God's law as an expression of God's love. God's love liberates us.

***God's liberating love liberates our love.***

*"God's love is in the preface to God's law.*
*Can we find love in the precepts of God's law?"*
*Lots of love there too.*

## God's Love Longs for Us 20:3–11

The first four commandments express God's longing for us.

1. *Worship me only.* God is saying, "I long for your loyalty."
2. *Worship me my way.* God is saying, "I long for your worship."
3. *Honor my name.* God is saying, "I long for your respect."
4. *Remember my day.* God is saying, "I long for your time."

Every marriage develops a set of unwritten rules as the husband and wife get to know one another's likes and dislikes. That doesn't turn the couple into lawyers. No, it helps them to be lovers. That's why God wrote out his rules—not because he wants to be our lawyer, but because he wants to be our lover.

***God longs for us, more than for our obedience.***

*"But what about the other commandments?"*
*Love leaps there too.*

## God's Love Looks After Us 20:12–17

Commandments 5–10 express God's care for us. Each one of them protects us from ourselves, protects us from others, and protects others from us. God's love looks after us.

***God's protective laws reveal protective love.***

*"It still seems very restrictive. Where's the love in all the restrictions?"*
*Love is restricted without restrictions.*

## God's Love Limits Us 20:18–26

Yes, God does set limits, but it's his love that is behind the limits. Just as I limit my eight-year-old son's screen time, so God limits our sin time (to zero). My limits and God's limits are expressions of fatherly love. In verses 18–26, God moves from boundaries for everyday life to boundaries for church life. He sets boundaries as to where, what, and how to worship. God's love limits us.

*A love without limits is a limited love.*

### Changing Our Story with God's Story

Can you see God's love in the law now? A love that liberates, a love that longs, a love that looks after us, and a love that limits us. It begins with loving liberation and ends with loving limitations. He liberates us from the danger of sin and limits us within the boundaries of his blessing. And within these boundaries he longs for us and looks after us. You don't want to miss out on that love, do you?

**Summary:** How can we experience God's love in God's law? *Love God's law as an expression of God's love and you'll experience more of God's love.*

**Question:** How does Jesus's teaching about the love of God in the law of God in John 14:15–17 encourage your obedience?

**Prayer:** Loving Lawgiver, give me love for your law so that I can enjoy your love in the law.

**Humans can abuse power to damage the weak, but God uses his power to deliver the weak.**

27

# The Defender of the Defenseless

## EXODUS 21:1–11

Big people often oppress small people. When people have power over others, they can abuse that power. You've probably seen that in school, in the workplace, and even in your own family. To some degree, we've all been victims of bullying, oppression, and abuse that make us feel defenseless and helpless.

*How can we defend and help the oppressed?* One of God's most beautiful character traits is his defense of the defenseless, his help of the helpless. God reveals his beautiful character in his care for the weak and abused in Exodus 21:1–11.

### God Frees the Captives 21:1–6

God hates slavery and loves freedom. God proved that by delivering the Israelites from Egyptian slavery, and reminded them of that in Exodus 19 and 20. God loves freeing captives. We see God's love for captives and his passion for freedom in Exodus 21's laws about slaves. There he issues rules to ensure that any Hebrew slave was to be released for no payment after six years.

However, God also recognized that some slaves would come to love masters who treated them and their families well and would want to stay in these circumstances. "But if the slave plainly says, 'I love my master, my wife, and my children; I will not go out free,' then his master shall bring him to God, and he shall bring him to the door or the doorpost. And his master shall bore his ear through with an awl, and he shall be his slave forever" (21:5–6). This permanent mark would be a testimony to the mutual love and commitment of both the master and the slave.

While powerful people sometimes use their power to oppress, the all-powerful God uses his power to free.

***Humans can abuse power to damage the weak,***
***but God uses his power to deliver the weak.***

*"How does God prevent abuse?"*
*He has laws for that too.*

## God Defends the Defenseless 21:7–11

In verses 7–11, God sets special protections for female slaves who would be especially vulnerable to abuse. God protected them from male slaves (21:7), from foreigners (21:8), and from abuse in her master's family (21:9–10). God does not condone fathers selling daughters into slavery. But knowing the tendencies of the human heart, God looked ahead, saw the potential for oppression and abuse, and got ahead of it with laws to defend and deliver from it. Isn't that beautiful? Isn't God beautiful?

Abused for many years by the American gymnastics team doctor, Larry Nasser, Rachael Denhollander showed the heart of God when she stood up against her abuser and the gymnastics establishment. Having secured the abuser's conviction, Rachael and her husband, Jacob, now campaign against abuse in every walk of life. That's a flesh-and-blood revelation of the heart of God, and it's beautiful to see.

If you are a victim of abuse, know that God stands ready to defend you, deliver you, and destroy your abuser.

***Bullying is terrifyingly ugly,***
***but defending the bullied is beautiful.***

## Changing Our Story with God's Story

As the perfect flesh-and-blood revelation of God, Jesus showed this same heart for the oppressed and abused, especially those spiritually oppressed and abused by their own sin. He said, "Truly, truly, I say to you, everyone who practices sin is a slave to sin. . . . So if the Son sets you free, you will be free indeed" (John 8:34–36). Jesus delivers us from our greatest bullies, oppressors, and abusers—Satan and our own sinful hearts.

**Summary:** How can we defend and help the oppressed? *Worship and imitate the God who frees captives and defends the defenseless.*

**Question:** How can you imitate God as the defender and helper of the oppressed today?

**Prayer:** Defender of the Defenseless, thank you for freeing me and defending me. Use me to free and defend others who are also weak and helpless, so that others will know what kind of God you are.

**God will never overpunish, but neither will he underpunish.**

28

# An Eye for an Eye

## EXODUS 21:12–36

Human justice tends to overpunish or underpunish. That's true not only in our courts but also in our workplaces, our families, and our other personal relationships. Sometimes we're too harsh; sometimes we're too soft. With overpunishing, the offender is punished too much. With underpunishing, the victim suffers all over again and evil is not deterred. Human justice is so faulty.

Like yourself, I've been the victim of painful injustice. I've been overpunished. I've been punished for things I did not do. I've seen evil go unpunished and the innocent punished when they should have been protected. But I've not been a perfect punisher either. I'm sure there are times when I've over- and underpunished.

*How can justice be administered in a way that avoids both extremes?* Let's turn to Exodus 21:12–36, where God gives us two principles of justice that help us avoid under- or overpunishing.

### Punish Exactly **21:12-36**

At the center of this passage is God's fundamental principle of justice, that is, the punishment must fit the crime. "If there is harm, then you shall pay life for life, eye for eye, tooth for tooth, hand for hand, foot for foot, burn for burn, wound for wound, stripe for stripe" (21:23–25). This exact justice demands that we avoid under- and overpunishment. If someone takes a life, we don't take a tooth from the guilty party. If someone punches someone else, we don't take the perpetrator's life from him. The punishment must fit the crime. Not too much, not too little.

***We must punish exactly because God will punish exactly.***

*"But are there ever special circumstances?"*
*Yes, let's note them.*

## Consider Mitigation 21:12-36

Although the center of this passage is God's first, fundamental, and inflexible principle of justice, all around it are various qualifications and conditions to be considered when administering justice:

- *Measure the motive* (*21:13–14*): Was the act deliberate and premeditated or not?
- *Value the victim* (*21:15–17*): What was the status of the victim and the relationship of the victim to the offender?
- *Count the cost* (*21:18–23*): How serious was the hurt, damage, or loss?
- *Research the responsibility* (*21:28–36*): Could the act have been avoided with more care and forethought?

All of these mitigating factors must be taken into account when applying God's fundamental principle of eye-for-eye justice so that no one is overpunished or underpunished.

***God will never overpunish,***
***but neither will he underpunish.***

## Changing Our Story with God's Story

This passage reveals God as the perfect Judge who administers perfect justice to all. If you've ever been a victim of crime or injustice, you know how imperfect most human justice is. That's why we love to worship the God who one day will administer perfect justice. Perfect justice is beautiful.

Nowhere is God's perfect justice more beautiful than at the cross of Christ, where he was perfectly judged in our place without any mitigation. He paid life for life, eye for eye, tooth for tooth, hand for hand, foot for foot, wound for wound, stripe for stripe. In doing so, he suffered God's justice for all his people until there was zero left to suffer. Jesus suffered God's full justice until he fully satisfied God's justice.

If Christ is not our hope, then we will suffer God's perfect justice for all eternity. But if Christ has satisfied justice, we can have satisfying hope of a satisfying eternity.

**Summary:** How can justice be administered in a way that avoids extremes? *Do eye-for-eye justice but keep an eye on motive, victim, cost, and responsibility, and remember with joy that God has perfectly judged the perfect Christ in your place.*

**Question:** How can you put right any injustice you have done?

**Prayer:** Just God, I love your justice, especially because you have exacted the justice I deserved on your Son, Jesus Christ, so that you would now be unjust if you ever condemned me.

**Sin promises profit, but it's a get-poor-quick scheme.**

29

# How to Become Debt Free

EXODUS 22:1–15

Many of us have had the shadow of excessive debt hanging over us at some point in our lives. Sometimes we end up in debt through no fault of our own (e.g., medical bills, house repairs, being defrauded). Other times it's the result of poor choices (e.g., taking on too much student debt). But, if we're honest, sometimes it's the result of our sinful choices (e.g., running up huge credit card bills for goods and services that we didn't need).

That latter kind of debt especially can produce a sense of bondage, helplessness, and hopelessness. In addition to mental health problems such as depression and anxiety, such debt can even damage physical health through migraines, heart disease, and reduced resistance to infections.[1]

This is why God uses sinful debt to teach us about the debt of sin. But he also points us to how we can get our sin-debt paid off, which is the worst debt of all. *How can we get our sin debt paid off?* Exodus 22:1–15 kindles hope in the greatest debtor.

## Sin Incurs Debt 22:1-15

"If a man steals an ox or a sheep, and kills it or sells it, he shall repay five oxen for an ox, and four sheep for a sheep" (22:1). When someone steals, God imposes a debt upon him. Here, that

1 Bill Fay, "The Emotional Effects of Debt," https://www.debt.org/.

debt was not just the value of the animal but also included lost income resulting from the theft. The thief stole one animal but had to pay back four or five times the value of the animal. Sin incurs debt, a debt far greater than any gain we might have hoped for from the sin.

***Sin promises profit,***
***but it's a get-poor-quick scheme.***

*"Can't I just forget my debt?"*
*Denial is a common response but not a wise one.*

## We Must Repay Debt 22:1-15

"He shall repay" (22:1). God demands repayment of debt. Indeed, if someone had no assets to pay his debt, he had to sell himself to pay it (22:3). What began as a sinful scheme to increase wealth resulted in greater loss and sometimes even slavery and poverty.

Later in the chapter, God sets out how disputed debt should be settled (22:7–13) and when there should be full restitution. God is clearly opposed to sinful debt or choosing to default on debt. The debt and any penalty must be paid.

***Sin promises to make us full,***
***but leaves a bill we must pay in full.***

## Changing Our Story with God's Story

By instilling a horror of sinful debt, God was instilling a horror of sin as a debt. He was teaching us that sin was a debt, that sin-debt must be repaid, and when it couldn't, the debtor forfeited his life.

How welcome therefore are Jesus's words when he taught his people to pray, "Forgive us our debts as we also have forgiven our debtors" (Matt. 6:12). Because of Jesus, it doesn't matter how deeply in spiritual debt we find ourselves. With his cross, he can pay our debt in full.

On the cross, Jesus was the greatest debtor the world has ever seen. By taking the sins of his people, he took the greatest debt in history. But the cross was also the scene of the greatest debt repayment ever. No wonder he celebrated when he paid off the last cent: *It is finished!*

***Jesus paid it all, all to him I owe.***

**Summary:** How can we get our worst debt paid off? *Seek Christ's forgiveness for your unpayable debts and enjoy celebrating "It is finished!"*

**Question:** How can you use this debt illustration to share the gospel with others?

**Prayer:** Rich and Generous God, thank you for showing me my debt of sin and for paying it in full at the cross. Help me to enjoy that my debt is finished and to invite others to apply for repayment too.

**When we're running, running, running, God's saying rest, rest, rest.**

Hear God's Story | Change Your Story | Tell the Story | Change Others' Stories

30

# Take the Year Off!

EXODUS 23:10–13

We all go through times when we're extra busy and rest is rare. The demands of work take over our life with little or no time off. But even in normal times, work can dominate our thinking so much that we forget to look after ourselves and others. God is squeezed out in the stress. *How can I find rest in restless times?*

In Exodus 23:10–13, God provided a special remedy for overwork or overthinking about work. It was this: take the year off!

## Rest in Your King 23:10–11

"For six years you shall sow your land and gather in its yield, but the seventh year you shall let it rest and lie fallow" (23:10–11). God commanded Israel to take a year off work every seventh year to help them remember that as their Maker—and as the Maker of the land—he had the royal right to dictate how they lived and worked the land. In the seventh year God prohibited them from sowing their fields, and allowed them to eat only what grew naturally with his blessing but without their effort. God was telling them to remember and rest in their King.

***We can run around as kings,***
***or we can rest in our King.***

*"But how would they eat?"*
*God would provide.*

## Rest in Your Provider 23:11

"The seventh year you shall let it rest and lie fallow" (23:11). What's the first thought you would have if someone told you not to work for a year and just rest up? "How will I buy food? How will I pay the mortgage? What about school expenses?" God's blessing on the sixth-year harvest and on the unsown and unworked fields in the seventh year would provide sufficient food to meet all of their needs (Lev. 25:6, 19–21).

The Israelites were just like us. Sure, their specific worries were different, but they would still worry about how to provide for their families. This, therefore, was a test; by resting themselves and their land, they would be resting in God's provision. God was telling them to remember and rest in their provider.

***When God says "I will provide," don't say "No, I will provide."***

*"Am I just to sit around doing nothing for a year?"*
*No, physical rest facilitates spiritual work.*

## Rest in Your Rester 23:11–13

While resting from physical work, God's people were to engage in spiritual work. It was a time to think about God—who he was, what he was like. They were to see the kindness and love of God in the rest year. "The seventh year you shall let it rest and lie fallow, that the poor of your people may eat; and what they leave the beasts of the field may eat" (23:11). God was showing his goodness in caring for the weakest in society and in the fields.

Verse 12's instructions about the Sabbath day also reveal God's desire to rest and refresh his people, the land, the poor, animals, servants, and immigrants. God was telling them to remember and rest in their rester.

***When we're running, running, running,***
***God's saying rest, rest, rest.***

### Changing Our Story with God's Story

Imagine you were to visit Israel at this time. When you cross the border, it's totally silent and still. No workers in the field, no animals plowing. You enter a village, and everyone is sitting happily talking with one another. They seem to have all the time in the world. You ask, "What's wrong?" Everyone laughs. "Nothing's wrong; everything is right. We're resting in our God's sovereignty, his provision, and his rest. Come on over and we'll tell you more."

Doesn't that remind us of the one who said, "Come to me, all who labor and are heavy laden, and I will give you rest. Take my yoke upon you, and learn from me, for I am gentle and lowly in heart, and you will find rest for your souls. For my yoke is easy, and my burden is light" (Matt. 11:28–30)?

**Summary:** How can I find rest in restless times? *Rest in your King, your provider, and your rester.*

**Question:** What can we do in our daily lives to find more rest and therefore find more God?

**Prayer:** God of Rest, I rest in you because you are my King, provider, and rester.

**Most generals lead from behind, but our great general leads from the front.**

31

# God Goes before You

EXODUS 23:20–33

Recently my church had a Missions Emphasis Sunday. We heard God's stirring call to go forward with the gospel to the ends of the earth. We heard what we should do, how we should do it, and why we should do it. We heard from two inspiring missionaries who have obeyed God's call and who have gone forward with the gospel into a closed country in Central Asia. It was instructive, inspiring, and energizing.

But then Monday came, and with it came fear and hesitation. Moving forward looked much more difficult and much less appealing. We're often afraid of going forward, especially when we're alone.

We fear opposition, and we fear the unknown. Fear, fear, fear. *How do I move forward?* In Exodus 23:20–33, God has a message that will give us confidence to move forward. God moves us forward by going forward before us.

## God's Angel Goes Before You 23:20–25

"Behold, I send an angel before you to guard you on the way and to bring you to the place that I have prepared. Pay careful attention to him and obey his voice; do not rebel against him, for he will not pardon your transgression, for my name is in him" (23:20–21).

*Angel* means "messenger," and here the messenger is the Son of God. At various points in the Old Testament, he took on angelic form, or human form, centuries before he took on human flesh in his incarnation. We know it's no ordinary angel or messenger because of the way God describes him in these verses. He is to be obeyed (23:21), he is Israel's general (23:21), he will bless Israel (23:25–26), and, above all, God says, "My name is in him" (23:21). You might have heard of a book and a film called *Gods and Generals*, but here the promise is *God* is our general.

***Most generals lead from behind,***
***but our great general leads from the front.***

*"OK, I'm not terrified now, but I'm still afraid."*
*God's fearfulness removes our fear.*

## God's Fear Goes Before You 23:27

"I will send my terror before you and will throw into confusion all the people against whom you shall come, and I will make all your enemies turn their backs to you" (23:27). God promised to work in the psychology of Israel's enemies. He says, "I'll go before you as an invisible psychologist with access to your enemies' hearts and minds, and I'll put fear and confusion there so that they will run away when you appear." God will terrify, confuse, and defeat our enemies.

***God removes fear from our hearts and puts it in his enemies' hearts.***

*"But I still feel so lonely. Are any other soldiers with me?"*
*Yes, but there's a sting in their tail.*

## God's Hornets Go Before You 23:28–32

God has already promised that his presence will be with his people and his terror will go before them, and now he promises an additional army of soldiers. "And I will send hornets before you, which shall drive out the Hivites, the Canaanites, and the Hittites from before you. I will not drive them out from before you in one year, lest the land become desolate and the wild beasts multiply against you. Little by little I will drive them out from before you, until you have increased and possess the land" (23:28–30). God sends hornets as soldiers as part of a slowly-but-surely strategy that will guarantee total and complete victory (23:31).

*A slowly-but-surely strategy ensures a complete and total victory.*

### Changing Our Story with God's Story

God doesn't stand behind us and push us forward. He goes forward with us and even before us. He commissions us and commits to be *with* us and even *before* us.

We find Jesus repeating similar words in Matthew 28:18–20. There he commissions us, his New Testament people, and commits to be with us always and everywhere. What a rare general! So brave, so strong, so encouraging, so present, so powerful, so victorious.

**Summary:** How do I move forward? *Go forward with confidence because God goes forward before us to secure victory.*

**Question:** Where is God calling you to go forward today?

**Prayer:** My God and General, help me to go forward because you go before me.

**God wants to be friends with us more than we want to be friends with him.**

32

# God Enjoys You

## EXODUS 24

How would you describe your relationship with God? Nonexistent? Distant? On-and-off? Mechanical? Functional? Love/hate? One-sided? None of these are very enjoyable, are they? Wouldn't you love to have a better, deeper, more enjoyable relationship with God? Of course you would. We'd all love that.

Well, I've got good news for you. We can actually be friends with God. That's right; friendship with God is possible and enjoyable. In fact, friendship with God is the most wonderful experience in the world.

But, you may ask, *how can I be friends with God?* Here are three surprising truths from Exodus 24 that I hope will encourage you to enter, or enter deeper, into friendship with God.

### God Wants Our Friendship 24:1

God invited Moses, Aaron, Nadab, Abihu, and seventy elders of Israel to "come up to the LORD" (24:1). He called them up to worship him but *from afar*. God expressed a desire for friendship but wanted to caution them that this was not like a buddy-buddy friendship. This was a holy friendship.

*God wants to be friends with us*
*more than we want to be friends with him.*

*"I don't want a long-distance relationship. I want a close friendship." The good news is that so does God, but he has to make it safe for us first.*

## God Secures Our Friendship 24:2–8

God wanted friendship with Israel, but he wanted it to be a safe and secure friendship. That's why he next removed the danger involved in sinful Israelites becoming friends with a holy God. In Moses, he provided a mediator, or a go-between (24:2–3). In the Book of the Covenant, he provided a guide for their relationship (24:4–7). And in the sprinkled blood, he provided forgiveness and cleansing: "Moses took the blood and threw it on the people and said, 'Behold the blood of the covenant that the Lord has made with you in accordance with all these words'" (24:8).

*God did everything possible to make his friendship possible.*

*"I enjoy being friends with God, but I'm pretty sure*
*God doesn't enjoy being friends with me."*
*That's where we're so wrong.*

## God Enjoys Our Friendship 24:9–18

Verses 9–11 contain some of the most astounding words in the whole Bible:

> Then Moses and Aaron, Nadab, and Abihu, and seventy of the elders of Israel went up, and they saw the God of Israel. There was under his feet as it were a pavement of sapphire stone, like the very heaven for clearness. And he did not lay his hand on the chief men of the people of Israel; they beheld God, and ate and drank. (24:9–11)

Let that sink in. They saw the God of Israel. They ate and drank with the God of Israel. In that culture, eating and drinking together was the ultimate proof and pleasure of friendship. God wanted to see them and be seen by them. God wanted to enjoy them and be enjoyed by them.

*God feasts on our friendship, so why do we starve ourselves of it?*

## Changing Our Story with God's Story

There is no greater proof that God wants our friendship, secures our friendship, and enjoys our friendship than the life and death of Jesus. Jesus puts New Testament flesh on the Old Testament bones of friendship. In the Lord's Supper he even provides a regular meal to renew our friendship. There we can see God. There we can eat and drink with God. There we can enjoy God's friendship through Jesus.

**Summary:** How can I be friends with God? *Respond to God's offer of safe, secure, and supreme friendship, and enjoy his joy in you.*

**Question:** How are you responding to God's offer to be your best friend today?

**Prayer:** My God and My Friend, thank you for being my best friend. Help me to be a best friend to others by introducing others to your friendship through Jesus.

**God lived with us and like us, so that we can live with and like God.**

Hear God's Story | Change Your Story | Tell the Story | Change Others' Stories

33

# God's Living Room

EXODUS 25:1–9

God made us because he wanted to live with us. He wanted us to do life with him. That's what we see in the garden of Eden. God and our first parents do life together.

But sin entered and ruined that relationship. Adam and Eve ran away from God and hid from him. And that's where the human race finds itself today, isn't it? We don't want to live with God. We don't know how to live with God. We don't know if he wants to live with us. *How can God and I live together?*

We get an answer in Exodus 25:1–9. After giving Israel the law, he got them to build a living room for him. Why? "Let them make me a sanctuary, that I may dwell in their midst" (25:8). Let's visit God's living room and learn about living with God.

## God's Living Room Is Holy 25:8

"Let them make me a sanctuary" (25:8). *Sanctuary* means a holy place. The holiness of God's sanctuary—the tabernacle—was reflected in and enhanced by its very design. For example, God set six circles of holiness around his living place, circles that got smaller and smaller as they got nearer the center of the tabernacle. The biggest circle had virtually no restrictions about who could be there. But as people got nearer the center and the circles got smaller, the restrictions on who could be there increased in number. The ever-increasing restrictions reminded the Israelites that God is holy and the nearer to God we get, the holier we must become.

***A holy place for God can be a scary place for us.***

*"That sounds a bit scary. I'm not sure I'd want to be in God's living room." That's where the second part of verse 8 is so welcome and welcoming.*

## God's Living Room Is Inviting 25:8

"Let them make me a sanctuary, that I may dwell in their midst" (25:8). God wants to live with us, which is why the tabernacle was frequently called "the tent of meeting" (Ex. 38:8, 30). It was God's way of living in the midst of Israel and meeting with Israel. "There I will meet with you, and from above the mercy seat . . . I will speak with you " (Ex. 25:22).

But it's not just that God wants to live with us; God wants to live like us. Israel lived in tents, so God lived in a tent. He lived with them, and he lived like them. He came right down to their level and lived in the desert as they did, in tents like they did. This was an incredible privilege for Israel. God living with them was amazing enough, but God living like them was awesome.

***God lived with us and like us,***
***so that we can live with and like God.***

### Changing Our Story with God's Story

All this was only a shadow of good things to come (Heb. 10:1). The good thing to come was Jesus. "The Word became flesh and *dwelt* [lit., *tabernacled, tented*] among us . . . full of grace and truth" (John 1:14). In Jesus, God lived with us and like us in an even more astounding manner. He was Immanuel, God with us (Matt. 1:23). He was "the true tent [tabernacle] that the Lord set up, not man" (Heb. 8:2). He camped among us, full of grace and truth! Let our mouths be full of praise and thanks. If we want to meet with God, Jesus is the only place in the universe we can do this. He is our sacred space, our sanctuary, our living room, our tabernacle.

**Summary:** How can God and I live together? *Live with God because he wants to live with you and has made it possible through Jesus Christ.*

**Question:** How will you live with God today?

**Prayer:** Living God, thank you for living with me through Jesus Christ. Use me to invite others into your living room, Jesus Christ.

**God's mercy seat was made for meeting mercy seekers.**

Hear God's Story | Change Your Story | Tell the Story | Change Others' Stories

34

# God's Favorite Chair

EXODUS 25:10–22

Most of us have a favorite chair. When we sit in it, it seems to fit us perfectly, as it's taken our shape over the years. It's where we relax and do our favorite activities like reading, watching sports, listening to music, and so on.

God instructed Israel to make him a favorite chair. It fit him perfectly, and it was where he loved to sit and do his favorite activity. *What is God's favorite chair?* As we read about it in Exodus 25:10–22, I think it will become your favorite chair as well.

## God's Throne Is Made of Mercy 25:21

Immediately after announcing his desire to meet with Israel, God answered what was probably their biggest question: How? How can we meet with God? How can God meet with us?

His answer was a portable throne of mercy. "You shall make a mercy seat of pure gold" (25:17). God instructed Israel to build him a throne, starting with an ark, a wooden box covered with gold (25:10–11). Inside it, they were to place a copy of the law. The box lid, also called the mercy seat, was made of gold (25:17). On either side of it were gold cherubim with wings overshadowing the mercy seat and eyes looking down at it with awe and wonder (25:17–20).

It was a beautiful throne placed in the very center of God's living room. God was saying to Israel, "This mercy seat is my favorite chair. Mercy fits me perfectly. It's where I'm happiest and where I do my favorite work." Yes, it's a throne, but it's a throne of mercy that covers the law.

*God's favorite chair is where he gives free favor.*

*"If mercy is God's favorite chair, what's his favorite activity?" Meeting those who need mercy.*

## God's Throne Is Made for Meeting 25:22

Because God's favorite chair was a throne of mercy, it could also be a throne of meeting. "There I will meet with you, and from above the mercy seat, from between the two cherubim that are on the ark of the testimony, I will speak with you about all that I will give you in commandment for the people of Israel" (25:22). God's favorite chair is mercy, and his favorite activity is meeting with sinners.

The fact that the mercy seat is a throne reminds us that it's a place of power. Mighty mercy, powerful patience, great grace, and unlimited love sit on that chair. No wonder the cherubim are in awe. God meets with sinners there.

God's people meet God there to hear God there. He calls us to his throne so that he can teach us his word and help us to apply the word to our lives.

*God's mercy seat was made for meeting mercy seekers.*

## Changing Our Story with God's Story

"But we no longer have God's favorite chair like Israel did. How can I get mercy and meet with God?" The good news is that we have something even better. The mercy seat was only in one place and only one person at a time could actually meet with God there.

But in the New Testament, wherever we are and whoever we are, we can access God's favorite chair. That's because Jesus Christ is God's personal mercy seat and meeting place. On the cross, to the astonishment of the watching cherubim, he covered the law with his blood then sat down on the throne of heaven surrounded by astonished and adoring cherubim. We can come to God's favorite chair by faith and with prayer for mercy.

**Summary:** What is God's favorite chair? *"Let us then with confidence draw near to the throne of grace, that we may receive mercy and find grace to help in time of need"* (Heb. 4:16).

**Question:** What keeps you from God's favorite chair? What draws you to God's favorite chair?

**Prayer:** My King, your favorite chair is my favorite chair because there I not only find mercy but find out more about mercy. Keep me there and teach me there.

God wants a fellowship-food relationship, not a fast-food relationship.

35

# God's Supper Table

## EXODUS 25:23–30

Forty percent of American families eat dinner together three or fewer times a week. Ten percent never eat dinner together at all. Even when families do sit down together, it's not for long. Sixty years ago, the average dinnertime was ninety minutes. Today it's less than twelve minutes. The average American eats one in five meals in the car, and the average family now spends nearly as much on fast food as they do on groceries.

We're losing out on many blessings with our fast-food, solo eating habits. Kids and teens who share family dinners three or more times a week are less likely to be overweight, are more likely to eat healthy food, do better in school, are less likely to engage in risky behavior, and have better relationships with their parents.

In *The Atlantic*, a journalist wrote: "The dinner table can act as a unifier, a place of community. Sharing a meal is an excuse to catch up and talk, one of the few times where people are happy to put aside their work and take time out of their day. After all, it is rare that we Americans grant ourselves pleasure over productivity."[1]

Given all this, it's not surprising that God's mobile home, the tabernacle, had a supper table in it. *What does God's table say to us?*

1 See Cody C. Delistraty, "The Importance of Eating Together," *The Atlantic*, July 18, 2014 and Molly Logan Anderson, "Sit Down Dinner: Rediscover the Lost Art of the Family Meal," *The State Journal Register*, April 20, 2010. https://www.sj-r.com/.

## God Wants Rich Fellowship 25:23–29

The table was inside the room called the Holy Place. It was gold-plated, had a gold rim all around it, and was set out with gold plates, dishes, and utensils. Beautiful curtains, embroidered with brightly colored cherubim, covered the walls. Opposite the table was a large golden lamp casting a soft light upon the scene, and just off to one side was an incense-burning altar that filled the room with fragrance. This isn't McDonald's! It's a rich, beautiful, and inviting setting for a meal. Who wouldn't want to eat there?

*God wants gold-standard fellowship, not to-go fellowship.*

*"Does God really want me at his table?"*
*Look closer at the golden table.*

## God Wants Personal Fellowship 25:30

What was on this supper table? There were twelve loaves of unleavened bread set out in two columns of six (see Lev. 24:5–9). The table was set for all the twelve tribes of Israel. God was saying, "I want fellowship with all the Israelites."

The bread was renewed every week by the priests. As Israel's representatives, they came into the Holy Place, ate the bread on the table, and replaced it with twelve freshly baked loaves. The bread was called "the bread of the Presence" (25:30), messaging that God wanted the twelve tribes to live in his presence. Even when Israel marched, the table was to remain set with the bread as it was carried. Israel was reminded that they were before God and with God continually.

*God wants a fellowship-food relationship,*
*not a fast-food relationship.*

## Changing Our Story with God's Story

It's no accident that Jesus said he was the bread of life, the bread of God which came down from heaven and gave life to the world (John 6:32–35).

In the Old Testament only the priests could eat as Israel's representatives, but now all of God's people are a royal priesthood (1 Pet. 2:9), and all may eat with Christ by eating of Christ (John 6:53–58). Christ is our supper table where we can enjoy rich and personal fellowship with God. God is saying, "I want to spend time with you. I want to get to know you, and I want you to get to know me. I want us to prioritize pleasure over productivity." When we sit at God's table, we're saying the same back to God.

**Summary:** What does God's table say to us? *Prioritize pleasure over productivity by using mealtimes to fellowship with one another and with God.*

**Question:** How can you increase the number, length, and quality of mealtimes with God?

**Prayer:** Fellowshiping God, thank you for the many times you've shared a meal with me. Help me to bring others to your happy table.

## You can't get life without light.

Hear God's Story | Change Your Story | Tell the Story | Change Others' Stories

36

# God's Lamp

EXODUS 25:31–40

Do you know anyone who enjoys darkness? Most of us don't like the darkness. We associate darkness with danger and death. Light, on the other hand, is safety and life.

The Bible goes even further and tells us that there's a darkness inside us that's no less dangerous or deadly. It's a moral and spiritual darkness that prevents us from seeing moral and spiritual truths about God. *How can we get light in our darkness?*

Let's use Exodus 25:31–40 to revisit the Holy Place in the tabernacle and study the golden lamp on the golden table.

## God Is the Light-Giver 25:31–40

The lamp was made from seventy-five pounds of gold. The base supported one main pipe, with six other smaller pipes branching out on either side of it, and lamps burning on each end. One of the priests' tasks was to keep the lamp burning so that it was never extinguished (Ex. 27:20–21).

God was saying to Israel, "I am your light-giver. I am your safety and security in a dark world. I will give you my light in a dark and dangerous world. But, more than that, I will shine not just around you but inside you. I will dispel your inner darkness with my light. I am the light-giver. That's far more valuable and far more beautiful than gold.

*God lightens and brightens*
*our world and our soul.*

*"What does this light produce?"*
*It produces life.*

## God Is the Life-Giver 25:31–40

The lamp was designed to look like a tree. "And there shall be six branches going out of its sides, three branches of the lampstand out of one side of it and three branches of the lampstand out of the other side of it; three cups made like almond blossoms, each with calyx and flower, on one branch" (25:32–33).

Each branch of the golden lamp was carved with shapes representing the three stages of life in an almond tree: bud, blossom, fruit. The entire thing was like a beautiful fruit-bearing tree. Without light, nothing grows and everything dies. God designed this treelike lamp to show that by being the light-giver, he was also the life-giver.

This tree pointed them backward to the tree of life forfeited by sin (Gen. 3:24) and forward to the tree of life, which would be enjoyed by grace in glory (Rev. 22:1–2).

***You can't get life without light.***

## Changing Our Story with God's Story

What New Testament verse does this combination of light and life remind you of? How about Jesus's words in the book of John: "I am the light of the world. Whoever follows me will not walk in darkness, but will have the light of life" (8:12). Jesus was saying that the golden lamp has come alive to give light and life to the world. He didn't light up just the Holy Place; he lit up the entire world. His coming made the world a brighter and better place, a safer and happier place.

He doesn't just give light to the world; he puts it inside his people also. They *will have the light of life*. It will give them moral and spiritual light so that they can see and understand God. As Paul said, "For at one time you were darkness, but now you are light in the Lord. Walk as children of light (for the fruit of light is found in all that is good and right and true), and try to discern what is pleasing to the Lord" (Eph. 5:8–10).

Christ is God's light giver and life giver. He is the light of the world and the tree of life who produces fruit in his people.

**Summary:** How does light come to a world of darkness? *God's living lamp gives light and life to your soul so you can be light and life to others.*

**Question:** Whose life will you shine God's light into today?

**Prayer:** Light-Giver and Life-Giver, let there be light and life in me so that I can be light and life to others.

**God gives a beautiful welcome into his beautiful presence.**

Hear God's Story | Change Your Story | Tell the Story | Change Others' Stories

37

# God's Curtains

## EXODUS 26

A few years ago, I was in a church that was home to many converted Roman Catholics. I asked the pastor what had drawn so many Roman Catholics to his church. He said he noticed a change when he started speaking about how Jesus is our connection to God.

These Roman Catholics had been told all their lives that they were disconnected from God and the only way to connect with God was through priests and the Roman Catholic Church. But they still felt disconnected from God. They were still asking, *"How do we connect with God?"* When this pastor started proclaiming Jesus Christ as our direct connection with God, his message resonated deeply with many Roman Catholics in that community. It is appealing, isn't it?

But such connection was not so easy, direct, or free in the Old Testament. Although God gave the tabernacle as a meeting place with Israel, a number of barriers existed that prevented direct connection with God. Among these barriers were a number of curtains, which we find in Exodus 26.

### God's Curtains Protect 26:12–14

God provided detailed instructions about various curtains he wanted in the tabernacle: the number, the color, the materials, the layers, the connectors, the position, the embroidery, and so on.

Partly, all of this detail was to protect the tabernacle from the weather. For example, the outside layer of the curtain was made from waterproof and windproof goatskins. But the curtains were also to protect the people from straying into God's presence unprepared. The curtains separated but they also protected.

***God protects us from ourselves and from himself.***

*"So, would any old curtains do?"*
*No, these were special curtains.*

## God's Curtains Beautify 26:1, 31

While the outer curtains were functional, the inside curtains were beautiful. They had beautiful colors (blue, purple, scarlet) and a beautiful design, with cherubim embroidered into them. When the priests entered this part of the tabernacle, they were surrounded by beauty.

***God gives a beautiful welcome into his beautiful presence.***

*"Can I see what's on the other side of the curtain?"*
*Let's try and see.*

## God's Curtains Hide 26:36

The curtains draped over the Holy Place and the Most Holy Place hid the furniture inside them from prying eyes. Sure, the priests could go in and come out to tell the people what was there and what each piece of furniture meant. But the people couldn't learn directly. The furniture was hidden from their eyes. This reminded them that the tabernacle was still shadow-truth. It revealed, but it also hid.

***God gives some truth to make us hunger***
***for more truth.***

### Changing Our Story with God's Story

We find a very different picture in the New Testament. There God rips curtains and removes them through Jesus Christ. The moment Jesus died on the cross, "the curtain of the temple was torn in two, from top to bottom" (Matt. 27:51). When Jesus's flesh was torn and shredded, so were God's curtains. Jesus is God's curtainless tabernacle through whom we can connect directly, freely, and safely with God in his beautiful presence. "Therefore . . . since we have confidence to enter the holy places by the blood of Jesus, by the new and living way that he opened for us through the curtain, that is, through his flesh, and since we have a great priest over the house of God, let us draw near with a true heart in full assurance of faith" (Heb. 10:19–22).

The more we see Christ as the great connector, the more we will have true hearts and assured faith.

**Summary:** How do we connect with God? *Connect with God through Christ the connector for protection, attraction, and connection.*

**Question:** Share this devotional with a Roman Catholic. What kind of response did you get?

**Prayer:** Christ the Connector, thank you for bringing God to me and me to God. Thank you for the cross, which tore down every barrier between me and you so that I can enjoy God's safe, beautiful, and nearer presence.

**Sin is too powerful for us, but God is too powerful for sin.**

Hear God's Story | Change Your Story | Tell the Story | Change Others' Stories

38

# God's Fireplace

## EXODUS 27:1–8

Have you ever wanted to meet with someone, but when you get your calendars out to arrange a date, it's almost impossible to find a time that suits both of you? You want to meet, and the other person wants to meet, but your different lifestyles, obligations, and schedules make it almost impossible. *"How can we ever meet with God?"* you might ask.

We see a similar difficulty in the tabernacle. The different pieces of tabernacle furniture said to the Israelites, "God wants to meet with you." But when they started walking toward the tabernacle to enter the front door, what's the first thing they saw? Blocking their way was a big metal altar with flames leaping out of it (Ex. 27:1–8).

God wanted to meet with them, and they wanted to meet with God, but there was a big obstacle in the way, raising the perplexing question, "How can we ever meet with God?" What message was he communicating to Israel and to us?

### The Altar Is Important 27:1–8

What's the first thing you see when you enter the grocery store? Usually it's a big promotional display of some kind, isn't it? It's what the store manager has decided to promote that week. Sometimes it's food, other times a drink or perhaps a toy. Whatever it is, the manager wants us to see it and buy it. By her arrangement and placement of the product, she's saying, "This is important. I want you to pay attention to this and hopefully pay for it too." The product may not have been on our shopping list, but the manager wants it to be first on our list.

So when we see that God gave the first and most prominent place to the metal altar, he was saying, "This is important. I want you to pause and pay attention to what I'm doing here."

***Dealing with sin may not be on our list, but it's first on God's list.***

*"Why was the altar so important?"*
*Because it was addressing a serious problem.*

## The Altar Is Serious 27:1–8

Most promotional displays are arranged to be attractive and enticing. Bright colors, fun pictures, happy signs, and clever messages are used to draw us in.

But that's not what the Israelites saw at the altar. Quite the reverse. It was a holy altar with a huge fire on it. Around it was the blood of animals and on it were burning animal carcasses. This was not a bright, cheery sight. What was happening here was serious and solemn. God was dealing with sin.

***God deals seriously with sin because we are serious sinners.***

*"Did it work? Was it effective?"*
*Yes and yes.*

## The Altar Is Powerful 27:1–8

The altar was made of wood and overlaid with bronze, a metal that is associated with strength and endurance (Deut. 28:23; Jer. 1:18; Rev.1:15). It also had a metal grating inside it, which supported the sacrifice while the fire consumed it. On each corner of the altar were metal horns, which Scripture often uses to represent strength. The metal, the grating, and the horns were all combining to send the message that whatever happens here is powerful and strong.

***Sin is too powerful for us, but God is too powerful for sin.***

## Changing Our Story with God's Story

God wants to meet us. We want to meet God. But there's an obstacle, a problem in the way: our sin. We can't remove that, but God can and does. How? The author of Hebrews points to Jesus's work on the cross and says, *We have an altar!* (Heb. 13:10).

God put the cross at the entrance to the Christian life and through it said this is important, this is serious, and this is powerful. It's important that we deal with sin, God deals with sin seriously, and God powerfully removes sin so that we can meet with him. We have an altar!

**Summary:** How can we ever meet with God? *Prioritize God's altar to access God's presence, and you'll enjoy God's powerful removal of the most serious sin.*

**Question:** What does the Old Testament altar teach you about the New Testament altar?

**Prayer:** Holy God, thank you for the cross-shaped altar that makes it possible for us to make and keep our appointments with you.

**We are pathetic,**
**but God is sympathetic.**

39

# What a Friend We Have in Jesus

## EXODUS 28–29

I love fishing for king salmon, but I was never very good at it until I found a guide. He not only helped me start catching but he kept me safe as well.

We also need a guide in our spiritual lives. How do we approach God and meet with God in a safe and rewarding way? *Who will guide us into God's presence?* In Exodus 28–29, God gave the Israelites priests to serve in this role in the tabernacle.

### A Priest Is Supportive 28:1–12

Skillful craftsmen engraved the twelve names of the tribes of Israel on two onyx stones that were sewn into the shoulders of his priestly garments. Why did they do this? Moses tells us: "And you shall set the two stones on the shoulder pieces of the ephod, as stones of remembrance for the sons of Israel. And Aaron shall bear their names before the LORD on his two shoulders for remembrance" (28:12). Through these engraved shoulder stones, the priest said to Israel, "I remember you, support you, and carry you before the Lord."

***We are weak, but God is strong.***

*"But does he love me?"*
*Good question. Here's a great answer.*

## A Priest Is Sympathetic 28:29–30

The priest also had a breastplate with twelve precious gemstones sewn into it, each with the names of the twelve tribes engraved on them. "Aaron shall bear the names of the sons of Israel in the breastpiece of judgment [i.e., decision, guidance] on his heart, when he goes into the Holy Place, to bring them to regular remembrance before the Lord" (28:29). He wore this when he prayed for guidance for the Israelites. Through these engraved gems on his chest, the priest said to Israel, "You are on my heart. I love you, and I will guide you."

***We are pathetic, but God is sympathetic.***

*"But can the priest survive in God's presence?"*
*He can, so we can.*

## A Priest Is Safe 28:31–35

It wasn't safe for most of the Israelites to enter God's Holy Place, but it was safe for the priests. To assure Israel that the priest was safe, God put golden bells on the end of his robe so that Israel could hear them when the priest went into the Holy Place. "And it shall be on Aaron when he ministers, and its sound shall be heard when he goes into the Holy Place before the Lord, and when he comes out, so that he does not die" (28:35). These bells said, "I am safe and well in God's presence."

***We are risky, but God is safe.***

*"But is he different?"*
*As different as he needs to be.*

## A Priest Is Sanctified 28:36–38; 29:1–44

On his head, the priest wore a turban with a gold plate engraved with "Holy to the Lord" (28:36). "It shall be on Aaron's forehead, and Aaron shall bear any guilt from the holy things that the people of Israel consecrate as their holy gifts. It shall regularly be on his forehead, that they may be accepted before the LORD" (28:38). This gold plate said, "I am your holy representative. When I offer your sacrifices and gifts to God, he accepts me, you, and them as holy." Exodus 29 gives us the details of the priests' consecration service.

***We are sinful to the Lord,***
***but the priest is holy to the Lord.***

### Changing Our Story with God's Story

Support, sympathy, safety, and sanctification. What an amazing guide! What a spiritual friend to have! But all of this pointed to God's final priest, God's great high priest, Jesus Christ. The whole book of Hebrews is devoted to showing us the superiority of Jesus as our spiritual guide (see Heb. 7:26–27; 8:1–6; 9:11–14, 24–28; 10:11–14). In him there is perfect support, sympathy, safety, and sanctification. What a friend we have in Jesus!

**Summary:** Who will guide me into God's presence? *Use God's strong, sympathetic, safe, and sanctifying spiritual guide to guide you safely and successfully into God's presence.*

**Question:** Why is Jesus such a perfect spiritual guide for you?

**Prayer:** My Heavenly Priest, your support, sympathy, safety, and sanctification encourage me to trust you in guiding me into God's presence.

**Our prayers feel worthless to us, but they're precious to God.**

Hear God's Story | Change Your Story | Tell the Story | Change Others' Stories

40

# The Perfume of Prayer

EXODUS 30:1–10, 22–38

"My prayers are so bad. *So what's the point of praying?*" Ever thought that? I have. I sometimes think, "My prayers have no value, my prayers have no beauty, and my prayers have no power." What's the effect of such thinking? It discourages and reduces prayer, doesn't it? If that's what we think of our prayers, we will not pray. But the Bible teaches us to think of prayer very differently, which produces very different results.

After a couple of chapters on the priests (Ex. 28–29), chapter 30:1–10 takes us back inside the tabernacle and shows us a second altar, the altar of incense, which was a symbol for prayer ascending to God (Ps. 141:2; Rev. 5:8; 8:3). In Luke 1:10 we read that when the priest was burning incense, the people were praying, signifying that prayer is the true incense.

## Prayer Is a Costly Perfume 30:1–3, 34–38

Unlike the altar for sacrifices which was covered with strong bronze, the altar of incense was covered with pure gold. It had a gold rim and four golden horns (30:3). The incense was made up of rare and precious ingredients (30:34–38). God was saying through the precious metal and precious ingredients, "Prayer is precious to me. I value it highly."

*Our prayers feel worthless to us,*
*but they're precious to God.*

*"But some costly perfumes smell horrible."*
*That's true, but it's not true of this perfume.*

## Prayer Is a Sweet Perfume 30:22–38

Three times the incense is described as sweet (30:22, 34). God thought up a recipe that would fill the Holy Place with the most beautiful fragrance, making it a beautiful place to pray and leaving a beautiful scent on the priests.

God was assuring Israel that their prayers were beautiful to him. They sent a scent to heaven. The place of prayer is a beautiful place. And prayer leaves a heavenly scent upon us.

***Our prayers are an ugly stench to us but a sweet scent to God.***

*"But what's the effect?"*
*Much more than you think.*

## Prayer Is a Powerful Perfume Ex. 30:1–10

Like the other altar, this had golden horns on the four corners (30:3), reminding Israel that though their prayers felt weak to them, they were powerful with God. The fact that the altar was to burn incense continually and forever (30:8) encouraged the people that their prayers lasted in God's presence long after they had prayed them. This altar had to be cleansed with blood every year (30:9–10), another reminder that their prayers were powerful only because they were covered in sacrificial blood.

***Our prayers can feel so powerless,***
***but sacrificial blood makes them powerful.***

## Changing Our Story with God's Story

Like everything in the tabernacle, the incense altar taught Israel present truths about God, but it also predicted a future Savior. The altar of incense therefore taught them valuable lessons about prayer but also pointed to a future that would make these truths even bigger and clearer.

That's exactly what Jesus did. He is the altar of incense in human form (John 14:13; Rev. 5:8; 8:3). It's through him and his blood that our prayers become precious, pleasing, and powerful before God. Now that will make us pray!

Here's how Charles Spurgeon put it: "Jesus stands ready to take every prayer of ours, however imperfect in knowledge, however feeble in expression, however marred with sorrow, and He presents the purified and perfected prayer with His own merit—and it is sure to speed. . . . There is such delicious sweetness in Christ to the Father that it effectually destroys the ill savor of anything that comes from us!"[1]

**Summary:** "My prayers are so bad. So what's the point of praying?" *Pray through Christ so that your prayers will be precious, pleasing, and powerful before God.*

**Question:** How do Christ's prayers for you change your prayers to God?

**Prayer:** Most High God, I offer you my lowly prayers in the costly, sweet, and mighty name of Christ, because I know that such prayers are precious, pleasing, and powerful with you.

1 Charles Spurgeon, *Spurgeon's Sermons*, vol. 29, no. 1,710, "Incense and Light" (1883), *Christian Classics Ethereal Library*, https://www.ccel.org/ccel/spurgeon/sermons29.xiii.html.

## Calculate your value by calculating your ransom.

Hear God's Story | Change Your Story | Tell the Story | Change Others' Stories

41

# I Won't Forget the Man Who Died

## EXODUS 30:11–16

"I'm proud to be an American, where at least I know I'm free."[1] My son Scot and I play this song and croak along with it every morning on our ride to his school. Whatever else is going on, it's good to remember our fundamental freedom. "At least I know I'm free." But are we? Sure, we're politically free; we're free citizens. But are we really free, fully free?

Not according to God. In his word, God teaches us that we are born in spiritual chains, under spiritual bondage (John 8:31–36). The devil has kidnapped us and claimed us as his own. How can we get free? The next lines in Lee Greenwood's song speak about those who died to make us free. *Can anyone pay a ransom to free us spiritually?* Let's study ransom in Exodus 30:11–16 to learn more about how God provides a ransom.

### A Ransom Recognizes Ownership 30:12–14

God instructed Moses to take a census of Israel. Each person twenty years and older was to give half a shekel as an offering to the Lord. God called this payment a ransom that saved them from the plague and spared their lives. When paying this, Israel would be reminded

1 Lee Greenwood, "God Bless the U.S.A," track 5, side 2, *You've Got a Good Love Cominn'*, MCA Nashville, 1984.

that now they were not their own but belonged to God, the God who held their health and their lives in his hand.

***We owe God because he owns us.***

*"But no one would pay a ransom for my little life, right?"*
*Wrong.*

## A Ransom Reflects Value 30:15

The value of every single life was reflected in the fact that the rich gave the same as the poor and that the poor were not exempted from paying despite their poverty. God valued each life equally.

***Calculate your value by calculating your ransom.***

*"What does life look like after the ransom is paid?"*
*It looks redeemed.*

## A Ransom Results in Freedom 30:16

"You shall take the atonement money from the people of Israel and shall give it for the service of the tent of meeting, that it may bring the people of Israel to remembrance before the LORD, so as to make atonement for your lives" (30:16). The ransom was an atonement and reminded Israel that God secured their freedom and therefore he was to be honored as their liberator.

***I'm humbled to be a Christian,***
***where at least I know I'm free.***

## Changing Our Story with God's Story

God was not only teaching Israel that, by God's grace, they belonged to God, they were valuable to God, and they were freed by God. He was also preparing vocabulary and concepts that he would use to teach his New Testament church about Jesus.

Jesus himself used this language and idea to explain who he was and what he was doing. "The Son of Man came not to be served but to serve, and to give his life as a ransom for many" (Matt. 20:28; see 1 Tim. 2:5–6; 1 Cor. 6:19–20). Today, we don't have to pay a cent toward the ransom. "Jesus paid it all, all to him I owe."[2]

Let's praise the Redeemer who paid our ransom with his own life, and in so doing said, "You're mine, you're valuable, and you're free."

**Summary:** Can anyone pay a ransom to free us spiritually? *Remember and honor the liberator who paid your ransom, and tell other captives about it too.*

**Question:** How does Christ's ransom change the way you view and use your body?

**Prayer:** Lord, thank you for accepting my liberator's ransom to free me from sin. Help me to pay him back with faith, love, and worship.

2 Elvina M. Hall, "Jesus Paid It All," 1865.

**Sin is love for mud, but God washes us with love.**

42

# God's Washroom

## EXODUS 30:17–21

Have you ever noticed how much little boys are attracted to dirt? If there's a muddy puddle, they go out of their way to jump in it. The other day I was hiking a path with my eight-year-old son. It had been raining, and I spent the whole time navigating my way around the ankle-deep mud. He spent the time navigating his way into and through the mud. Thankfully, this phase doesn't last forever, and most boys join the rest of the human race in their mid- to late-twenties!

Most of us hate getting dirty, and we go to great lengths to avoid dirt or wash it off as soon as we can. Dirt makes us feel horrible and look horrible. That's why a bath or shower is so welcome and enjoyable, so refreshing and renewing.

But what about moral dirt? The Bible pictures sin as a dirt problem. Do we see that? Do we feel that? Do we hate that? If so, do we want to get cleaned up? *How do we wash our sin away?*

Let's see how serious this need for washing is and how God solves this problem in Exodus 30:17–21.

### God Provides Bodywashing 30:17–20

Before the priests could serve God, they had to wash at a bronze bath filled with water.

Two main washings occurred at this bath. The first was a one-time full-body washing when priests were first ordained and installed (Ex. 29:4). The second was daily feet- and handwashing (Ex. 30:19–21). God provided ample cleansing, so there was no excuse for a priest to be dirty and so excluded from God's presence. Sin dirties and disconnects, but God cleanses and reconnects.

***Sin is love for mud, but God washes us with love.***

*"This washes my body, but can it wash my soul?"*
*No, but something else can.*

## God Points to Soul-Washing 30:17–20

In Exodus 38:8, we read that Moses "made the basin of bronze and its stand of bronze, from the mirrors of the ministering women who ministered in the entrance of the tent of meeting."

It looks like these godly women were giving up their focus on outward cleanliness and beauty to focus primarily on inward cleansing and beauty. They brought their mirrors, symbols of personal beauty and glory, and dedicated them to God's beauty and glory.

Moses made the base of the bath out of these mirrors so that the priests would have mirrors to use when they were washing. It must have been nerve-wracking to be a priest: "They shall wash with water, *so that they may not die*. They shall wash their hands and their feet, *so that they may not die*" (Ex. 30:20–21). The mirror helped them to see the dirt to wash off. And when they saw their own reflection, they must have also longed for the Messiah priest who would be perfect and who didn't need such personal washing.

***Mirror, mirror, on the base,***
***help us see Christ's glorious face.***

## Changing Our Story with God's Story

Jesus is the priest the mirrors pointed toward (John 17:19; Heb. 7:26–28). He is the perfect priest. Examine him from every angle, and you will find him flawless. He has clean hands and a pure heart, and has never lifted his heart to vanity (Ps. 24:3–4). He provides a one-time washing in our initial regeneration (Titus 3:5) and daily washing in sanctification (John 13:10; 15:3; 1 John 1:9).

**Summary:** How do we wash our sin away? *Praise God for providing Jesus Christ as our perfect priest, and enjoy the refreshment of his daily soul-washing.*

**Question:** Who can you encourage to turn from sin's mud to Jesus's love today?

**Prayer:** Washer and Cleanser, thank you for showing me my dirt as well as Christ's refreshing ability to wash it away with his blood.

**God is known through preaching and plumbing.**

Hear God's Story | Change Your Story | Tell the Story | Change Others' Stories

43

# The Beauty and Dignity of Manual Labor

EXODUS 31:1–11

Some people look down on manual labor and the trades today. So-called "headwork" is elevated and "handwork" is devalued. It's then a small step from demeaning manual work to demeaning manual workers. Manual workers often feel they and their work are not valued in our culture.

In a culture that doesn't value manual work, it can be easy to think that God doesn't value manual work and that such work is not worthy or useful in God's eyes. But *how does God view manual work?* In Exodus 31:1–11, God helps us to reassess the dignity, value, and spirituality of manual work, with many positive spiritual consequences.

## Manual Labor Is the Gift of God 31:1–11

God had instructed Moses how to make the tabernacle. Moses had written it down and drawn up the plans. But what now? They had to actually make it. Moses had been educated in elite Egyptian schools and was equipped to write books and organize a nation. But he didn't have all the necessary manual skills to build a tabernacle. Even if he had some skills, it wasn't his divine calling.

That's when God steps in and says to Moses. "See, I have called by name Bezalel the son of Uri, son of Hur, of the tribe of Judah, and I have filled him with the Spirit of God, with ability and intelligence, with knowledge and all craftsmanship, to devise artistic designs, to work in gold, silver, and bronze, in cutting stones for setting, and in carving wood, to work in every craft. And behold, I have appointed with him Oholiab, the son of Ahisamach, of the tribe of Dan. And I have given to all able men ability, that they may make all that I have commanded you" (31:2–6).

God called and equipped Bezalel and Oholiab, no less than he called Moses. God traced all manual skills to his calling, his gifting, and his Spirit. Does that not change the way you view yourself and your work?

*Manual work is spiritual work.*

*"Why does God give manual skills?"*
*To give back to him.*

## Manual Labor Glorifies God 31:1–11

If you're tempted to look down on manual work, remember that God was the first manual laborer. He made Adam from dust and Eve from Adam's rib. He made things out of things. Also, the first job God created was gardening. Bezalel is the first person that Scripture records as being filled with the Spirit, and it's to help him make stuff. We also remember that the Son of God was a carpenter for most of his life, a job to which he was divinely called and for which he was divinely gifted.

As the vast variety of manual skills are used, we see God's varied skills and abilities through them. We also see God's massive mind. Exodus 31:3 says that when God gave his Spirit, he also gave intelligence, knowledge, and craftsmanship. In other words, manual work is knowledge work too.

Manual skills reveal God's beauty. Although a large part of the tabernacle's design was about daily practicalities, some of God's design choices were simply about beauty.

Moses's preaching *and* Bezalel's and Oholiab's designing, cutting, nailing, and lifting resulted in God being better known and honored.

*God is known through preaching and plumbing.*

## Changing Our Story with God's Story

If God has gifted us with manual skills, it's because he sees a need we can meet that no one else can. If he's given us gifts like Bezalel's and Oholiab's, we don't try to be a Moses. And if we have Moses-type gifts, we encourage and value the Bezalels and Oholiabs. Both the church and the world need all of God's gifts.

Let's thank God for these gifts and by his Spirit put them to work to glorify him today by mirroring his skills, intelligence, beauty, and excellence in all that we do. If we do our God-given work, with God's help and for God's glory, we are worshiping him in, through, and with our work.

**Summary:** How does God view manual work? *Lift up manual work to lift up God in your mind, heart, and daily work. You will dignify your work and glorify God.*

**Question:** How will this change the way you work or view other workers?

**Prayer:** Giver of Every Good and Perfect Gift, thank you for the gifts of manual labor, which you use to dignify people and glorify yourself.

# God works for our rest.

Hear God's Story | Change Your Story | Tell the Story | Change Others' Stories

44

# God Works for Our Rest

EXODUS 31:12–18

We just learned about working for God, but we also need to learn about resting in God. As we have worked our way through Exodus, we have seen how God used everything to teach Israel about who he is. Nothing happened by chance, but rather God organized providence, people, and places so that Israel could learn who God was. The same goes for his Sabbath command in Exodus 31:12–18. What does the Sabbath teach us about God?

## The Sabbath Says God Is Important 31:12–14

After giving Israel so many laws, God prioritizes one of them. "Above all you shall keep my Sabbaths" (31:13). Why "above all"? Because if Israel gave up this command, all the others would quickly follow.

God emphasized the importance of this command by saying, "This is a sign between me and you" (31:13). Like all signs, the Sabbath was given to warn them, to keep them on the right path, and to direct them safely to their destination.

God then underlined the importance of the Sabbath by calling his people to obey it "throughout your generations" (31:13) and "throughout their generations as a covenant forever" (31:16).

And just in case they were still in any doubt, God highlighted the importance of the Sabbath by adding the sanction of death for any who profane it (31:14, 15).

***God is serious about the Sabbath***
***because he wants people to be serious about him.***

*"Why was it so important?"*
*Because it taught them that God is holy.*

## The Sabbath Says God Is Holy 31:13–15

The holiness of the day was communicated in three ways. First, God said he gave his people the Sabbath so that they " may know that I, the Lord, sanctify you" (31:13). It was a sign that separated them from the rest of the world and said, "My people are different." Next, God said, "You shall keep the Sabbath, because it is holy for you" (31:14). And finally, it wasn't just a day for rest but a day of "solemn rest, holy to the Lord" (31:15).

***The Sabbath separates us from sin***
***and moves us toward holiness.***

*"Has God given any example to help with this?"*
*Yes, he gave himself.*

## The Sabbath Says God Is Our Model 31:16–17

The sign of the Sabbath ultimately pointed to God as an example to follow. "It is a sign forever between me and the people of Israel that in six days the Lord made heaven and earth, and on the seventh day he rested and was refreshed" (31:17). God wasn't telling them to do something he didn't do himself. No, the Sabbath was a pointer to what God did on six days and didn't do on the seventh day. He didn't need to rest but chose to do so to encourage his people who do need it. In doing so he revealed himself as the one who worked for his people and then rested and refreshed his people. God's work was followed by his and his people's rest.

*God works for our rest.*

## Changing Our Story with God's Story

The Sabbath says God is important, God is holy, and God is our model. Praise God for this sign that he has given us for our spiritual benefit. And just in case we think that the New Testament has somehow eliminated this sign, Jesus reminded the Pharisees that he (not they) is Lord of the Sabbath (Matt. 12:8), and it was made to benefit people not burden them (Mark 2:27). He still calls laborers to rest in him (Matt. 11:28). While some of the smaller details have changed, the Lord's claim on the day remains, and its message remains the same. God is important, God is holy, and God is our example.

**Summary:** What does the Sabbath teach us about God? *Use the Sabbath given by God to prioritize God, separate to God, and enjoy rest in God.*

**Question:** What does your weekly rest day say about God?

**Prayer:** Lord of the Sabbath, thank you for using the Sabbath to bless me. Help me to use it to be a blessing to others.

# God’s promises are our prayers.

Hear God’s Story | Change Your Story | Tell the Story | Change Others’ Stories

45

# A Persuasive Prayer for the Backslidden

EXODUS 32:1–14

A Christian we know and love falls into a serious sin or even a pattern of immorality. We get angry with him and decide to stop praying for him. He's disappointed us and therefore we let him go; we turn our attention to others more faithful and godly. But *how should we pray when we hear that a Christian has committed a terrible sin?*

Let's ask Moses. While he was meeting with God, Aaron had led God's people into worshiping a golden calf. God saw what was happening and announced his intention to judge them: "I have seen this people, and behold, it is a stiff-necked people. Now therefore let me alone, that my wrath may burn hot against them and I may consume them, in order that I may make a great nation of you" (32:9–10). Moses's response provides us with a model prayer for backslidden Christians.

## Remind God of His Salvation 32:11

Moses reminded God of his past salvation to ensure Israel's present salvation: "Moses implored the LORD his God and said, 'O LORD, why does your wrath burn hot against your people, whom you have brought out of the land of Egypt with great power and with a mighty hand?'" (32:11).

*God's past salvation guarantees present and future salvation.*

*"What about God's relationship to his people?"*
*We can remind God of his covenant.*

### Remind God of His Covenant 32:11–12

Twice Moses reminded God of his covenant relationship to Israel. Twice he says they are "your people." It's a bold argument to make. "You can't do this, because they are yours."

***A bold prayer is a persuasive prayer.***

*"What about all the people mocking the fallen Christian?"*
*We can plead that too.*

### Remind God of His Enemies 32:12

"Why should the Egyptians say, 'With evil intent did he bring them out, to kill them in the mountains and to consume them from the face of the earth'?" (32:12). Moses cared for Israel, but he cared even more for God's glory. He could not bear the thought of God's reputation being tarnished and trashed by God's enemies.

***Turn the ungodly's words into godly prayers.***

*"Can we plead God's promises too?"*
*That's where Moses finishes.*

### Remind God of His Promises 32:13

"Remember Abraham, Isaac, and Israel, your servants, to whom you swore by your own self, and said to them, 'I will multiply your offspring as the stars of heaven, and all this land that I have promised I will give to your offspring, and they shall inherit it forever'" (32:13). Moses pled that God had made great promises, public promises, and repeated promises to Israel.

***God's promises are our prayers.***

## Changing Our Story with God's Story

Moses's prayer is full of tenderness and truth. His heart is full of compassion, and his mouth is full of arguments. He pleads his case and begs God to "turn from your burning anger and relent from this disaster against your people" (32:12). And wonderfully, "the Lord relented from the disaster that he had spoken of bringing on his people" (32:14). This doesn't mean that God changed his mind or corrected a mistake. It simply means that to encourage prayer, God allows himself to be seen as persuadable and responsive to prayers that are full of love and full of logic.

This prayer of Moses the mediator and its powerful effect is an audible example of the inaudible prayers of Christ our mediator as he also pleads for each of us as we sin and stumble along the way. Jesus's love-filled heart and logic-filled lips remind God of his salvation, his covenant, his enemies, and his promises. And, thank God, he always persuades and prevails.

**Summary:** How should we pray when we hear that a Christian has committed a terrible sin? *Count the number of times Christ has prayed for you when you have backslidden to encourage you to pray for others who are in a similar situation.*

**Question:** What backslidden Christian are you praying for?

**Prayer:** Savior, Covenanter, Conqueror, and Promiser, because of who you are, help backslidden Christians become who they should be.

Jesus was blotted out so we could be written into God's book of life.

46

# Punishing Sin and Praying for Sinners

EXODUS 32:15–35

We tend to go to extremes when dealing with sin. We can excuse it too easily or we can execute too harshly. That's true in our responses to sin in ourselves, in our families, in our friendships, in our churches, in our workplaces, and in our judicial system. Whether we excuse it too easily or execute too harshly, the end results are the same. We add sin to sin, we do no good to the sinner, and we do not glorify God.

*How should we respond to serious sin?* In Exodus 32:15–35, we can observe and learn from Moses's response to the Israelites' sin of idolatry. He punished sin and prayed for sinners.

## God's Mediator Punishes Sin 32:15–29

When Moses saw Israel's idolatry, "Moses' anger burned hot, and he threw the tablets out of his hands and broke them at the foot of the mountain. He took the calf that they had made and burned it with fire and ground it to powder and scattered it on the water and made the people of Israel drink it" (32:19–20).

Moses then confronted Aaron for his failed leadership, but Aaron blamed the people and even the golden calf for what happened (32:21–24)! Having dealt with the calf and with Aaron, Moses turned to deal with the people who by this point had descended into shameful chaos and disorder (32:25).

He cried out, "Who is on the Lord's side? Come to me" (32:26). When only the Levites came to his side, he armed them with swords and commanded them to execute God's judgment upon the people. By the end of the day, three thousand were dead (32:27–28). If any Levites had any doubt that this was God's will, Moses dispelled their doubts with these words: "Today you have been ordained for the service of the Lord, each one at the cost of his son and of his brother, so that he might bestow a blessing upon you this day" (32:29). God's future blessing depended upon their faithful dealing with sin.

***Sin must be punished if sinners are to be blessed.***

*"That's scary. How can any sinner ever know God?"*
*Thankfully, God provides a mediator.*

## God's Mediator Prays for Sinners 32:30–35

"The next day Moses said to the people, 'You have sinned a great sin. And now I will go up to the Lord; perhaps I can make atonement for your sin'" (32:30). He combined condemnation of sin with the hope of forgiveness. He does the same in his prayer to God. "Alas, this people has sinned a great sin. They have made for themselves gods of gold. But now, if you will forgive their sin—but if not, please blot me out of your book that you have written" (32:31–32).

It's a beautiful combination, isn't it? He confesses their sin, he pleads for forgiveness, and he even offers to be judged instead of the people to secure their forgiveness. Even though Moses had not sinned this sin, he was willing to be judged as if he had, to save those who really had.

God accepted the confession, rejected Moses's offer of substitution, and announced additional chastisement of the sin. But he also assured them of his presence going forward and that he would take them to the promised land (32:33–35).

***Jesus was blotted out so we could be written into God's book of life.***

## Changing Our Story with God's Story

In Deuteronomy 18:15, God promised that the future final mediator would be like Moses. Israel was to look for someone who punished sin and prayed for sinners. We now know this was Jesus, but he took it a step further by *being punished* for sin and praying for sinners. He forgave sin by being blotted out of God's book. Though he had never sinned, he was judged as if he had. He glorified God's holiness and dealt with our sinfulness. What a Savior! What a salvation!

**Summary:** How should we respond to serious sin? *Come to God through his perfect mediator, who was punished for our sin and prayed for sinners like us.*

**Question:** How does this change the way you deal with sin in yourself and in others?

**Prayer:** My Mediator, thank you for taking the punishment I deserve and praying for me. Help me to point other sinners to your sacrifice and prayers.

**God's absence makes us restless, but God's presence gives us rest.**

Hear God's Story | Change Your Story | Tell the Story | Change Others' Stories

47

# God's Absence Is Our Terror

## EXODUS 33:1–17

From 2000 to 2003 I pastored a congregation that did not have a church building. Despite the unusual and rather dilapidated surroundings, God's presence was evidently and palpably with us. Throughout those years, we were saving up for our own church building. God moved the hearts of his people to give generously, and within three years the new church was ready for opening.

The last Sunday worship in the town hall was a nervous occasion. We had been so blessed by God there that many of us were reluctant to move into our beautiful new church. *What if God leaves us?* That was the unspoken question on everyone's mind. I therefore preached on Exodus 33, where Moses pled for God's presence to go forward with God's people.

### God's Presence Can Be Withdrawn 33:1–6

In Exodus 32, God had punished Israel for worshiping a golden calf. He was so angry with the people that in Exodus 33 he announced to Moses that he would send an angel before them into the promised land, but because of their sins he himself would not go with them in the pillar of cloud and of fire. He would be with them indirectly through his angel, but not in such a special, direct, and visible way.

*God's presence may be reduced, but it is never removed.*

*"So, did Moses just settle for that reduced presence of God?"*
*Not at all; he could never settle for that.*

## God's Presence Can Be Pled For 33:7–16

We might have given up at that point, but not Moses. God's mediator went into God's meeting place, a place he knew well. There, God would come down in a cloud and "speak to Moses face to face, as a man speaks to his friend" (33:11).

That's when God's mediator went to work, pleading with the Lord to reverse his pronouncement. He boldly presented his case for God's presence with a number of arguments: you and I are friends; you've shown me great grace in the past; this nation is your people; and without you no other nation will know we are your special people (33:12–13, 16).

***God's mediator is face-to-face with God, and friend to friend with God.***

*"So how did God respond?"*
*With a promise of restoration.*

## God's Presence Can Be Restored 33:14–17

In response, God promised a restoration of his presence. "My presence will go with you, and I will give you rest" (33:14). But Moses wanted a double promise and continued to plead: "If your presence will not go with me, do not bring us up from here" (33:15). He was basically saying, "I'm not moving without you." He'd rather stay in the wilderness with God than enter the promised land without God. That's how precious God's presence was to Moses.

God gave Moses the extra security he craved by answering, "This very thing that you have spoken I will do, for you have found favor in my sight, and I know you by name" (33:17).

***God's absence makes us restless,***
***but God's presence gives us rest.***

## Changing Our Story with God's Story

We can identify with Moses's craving for God's presence and dreading the loss of it, can't we? The congregation I pastored would have stayed in the ugly town hall with God rather than gone to a beautiful new church without him. But thankfully we didn't have to choose because God graciously fulfilled his promise again in a wonderful way: "My presence will go with you and I will give you rest."

We were depending not on Moses to be our mediator but on Jesus Christ, who speaks to his Father face-to-face as a man speaks to his friend. Through him God is with us and gives us rest.

**Summary:** What if God leaves us? *Plead for God's presence in your life and be prepared to give up anything to have it and not lose it.*

**Question:** How do you know if God is with you in your daily life?

**Prayer:** Ever-present God, give me a constant sense of your presence, so that I can have a constant sense of your power.

# The goodness of God is the glory of God.

Hear God's Story | Change Your Story | Tell the Story | Change Others' Stories

48

# God's Goodness Is His Glory

EXODUS 33:18–34:7

When we hear someone's name, a picture pops up in our mind. That pop-up picture is what we think of first when we think of someone. That picture is usually the person's defining characteristic. It's a snapshot summary. It might be a smiling picture, a frowning picture, a stressed picture, a kind picture, or a scary picture. Whatever it is, it reveals what we think of the person, how we speak to her, respond to her, and if we want to be with her.

*What picture comes into your mind when you think about God?* Anger? Justice? Distance? Coldness? Judgment? Softness? Weakness? Whatever it is, that pop-up picture of God defines your relationship with God. It impacts and influences everything in your life.

What does God want us to think about when we think about him? In Exodus 33:18–34:8, we find a surprising and inspiring answer.

## God's Goodness Is His Glory 33:18–23

After God assured Moses that he would personally go with Israel, Moses said, "Please show me your glory" (33:18). Moses was asking God to show him his defining characteristic, what he wanted people to think of when they thought of God. In essence, Moses said, "Show me the right pop-up picture. Show me the image you want me to carry with me as we travel to the promised land."

God's answer is stunning: "I will make all my goodness pass before you and will proclaim before you my name 'The Lord'" (33:19). He effectively said, "My glory, my defining characteristic, is my goodness. That's what I want you to think of when you think of me. That's the image I want you to carry with you in life."

It was such a glorious image, such a bright and astounding picture, that God had to hide Moses in a cave so that when his goodness passed by, it would not blind Moses with its brilliance (33:20–23).

***The goodness of God is the glory of God.***

*"What does God's goodness mean?"*
*We find its meaning in the gospel.*

## God's Goodness Is Our Gospel 33:19–34:7

In Exodus 33:19 God promised he would show Moses his glorious goodness, and then said: "I will be gracious to whom I will be gracious, and will show mercy on whom I will show mercy." Then in Exodus 34 God passed before Moses and proclaimed his goodness, "The Lord, the Lord, a God merciful and gracious, slow to anger, and abounding in steadfast love and faithfulness, keeping steadfast love for thousands, forgiving iniquity and transgression and sin" (34:6–7).

God was saying, "My goodness is undeserved, patient, abundant, truthful, sovereign, and saving." God's goodness is our gospel. But it's a goodness that demands a response. He went on to say that he "will by no means clear the guilty, visiting the iniquity of the fathers on the children and the children's children, to the third and the fourth generation" (34:7). The saving goodness of God is available, but for those who do not want or appreciate his goodness, he will not clear their guilt.

*God's goodness is our gospel.*

## Changing Our Story with God's Story

We find an even better picture of God's glorious goodness in the New Testament. At Calvary, he made all his goodness pass before us and explained his name, "the LORD." In the death and resurrection of Jesus, God proclaimed, "I will be gracious to whom I will be gracious, and will show mercy on whom I will show mercy. The LORD, the LORD, a God merciful and gracious, slow to anger, and abounding in steadfast love and faithfulness, keeping steadfast love for thousands, forgiving iniquity and transgression and sin."

As Moses bowed in worship in the cave, let's bow in worship at the cross for the glorious gospel of God's goodness.

**Summary:** What picture comes into your mind when you think about God? *Whenever you think of God, think first and most of his glorious goodness, especially as it was proclaimed at the cross.*

**Question:** How can you help others change their pop-up picture of God?

**Prayer:** Good God, thank you for proclaiming your goodness to me at the cross. Help me to proclaim your goodness, which you showed through the cross, to others.

# Freewill giving flows from free-grace getting.

Hear God's Story | Change Your Story | Tell the Story | Change Others' Stories

# 49

# Freely Gotten, Freely Giving

## EXODUS 35–36

*How do we increase giving to the church?* The church has three main funding methods. The first is to *force* people with verbal and emotional manipulation. The second way is to *fool* people, promising them if they give a dollar, God will give them back a million dollars. The third way is *freely*, where we leave it to God to work in people's hearts so that they give for the right reasons and in the right way. We have a beautiful example of that in Exodus 35–36.

### Generosity Is God-Centered 35:4–19

In Exodus 25–34, God provided Israel with the plans for the tabernacle and everything in it. Chapter 35 fills the funding gap with a beautiful story of how the Lord moved the hearts of the Israelites to provide the funding for the tabernacle.

First, Moses was careful to highlight that he was not asking for anything for himself. "Take from among you a contribution to the LORD" (35:5). Second, he wanted their contribution to the Lord to come from a generous heart: "Whoever is of a generous heart, let him bring the LORD's contribution" (35:5). He did not want it to be given grudgingly but generously; not out of law but out of love. Third, he gave a range of options. Some could give materials to the Lord (35:5–9), and some could give labor to the Lord (35:10–19).

***We're giving into the Lord's hands not into people's hands.***

*"If we are giving to God, how does God help us to give?"*
*He helps us to give with his giving.*

## Generosity Is God-Motivated 35:20–29

When God delivered the Israelites from Egypt, he moved the Egyptians to shower upon them gold, silver, and many other jewels and materials as they departed (Ex. 12:35–36).

When Moses asked these recent slaves to donate some of it to the Lord, they came, "everyone whose heart stirred him, and everyone whose spirit moved him, and brought the LORD's contribution to be used for the tent of meeting, and for all its service, and for the holy garments" (35:21). Five times we're told they were of a willing heart or their hearts stirred them or their hearts moved them (35:20–29).

What explains this beautiful example of how God can move the most unlikely people to incredible generosity? Gratitude. The visual theology in the tabernacle plans had just reminded them of all that God was and all that God had done. After hearing the plans and being reminded of the mercies of God, they were moved to give generously.

***Freewill giving flows from free-grace getting.***

*"What was the result of this giving?"*
*God was honored.*

## Generosity Is God-Glorifying 36:1–7

The people gave so much that the craftsmen couldn't get on with the actual work (36:5). Eventually Moses banned the people from giving any more materials (36:6), and "the people were restrained from bringing, for the material they had was sufficient to do all the work, and more" (36:6–7). Their more-than-sufficient giving mirrored God's more-than-sufficient giving.

***A giving people reveal a giving God.***

### Changing Our Story with God's Story

This is like an Old Testament Pentecost. In Acts 2, we read of what happened when God gave his Spirit:

> And all who believed were together and had all things in common. And they were selling their possessions and belongings and distributing the proceeds to all, as any had need. And day by day, attending the temple together and breaking bread in their homes, they received their food with glad and generous hearts, praising God and having favor with all the people. And the Lord added to their number day by day those who were being saved." (2:44–47)

Wouldn't you like to see something like this again?

**Summary:** How do we increase giving to the church? *Be moved by the generosity of God to give generously to God for the glory of God.*

**Question:** How can you increase your own giving?

**Prayer:** Giving God, give freely and fully of your Spirit, as you have done before, and I will give myself, and all that I have, freely and fully to you.

**When God lives with us, he never leaves us.**

Hear God's Story | Change Your Story | Tell the Story | Change Others' Stories

50

# The Ever-Living, Never-Leaving God

## EXODUS 40:33–38

What are our basic spiritual needs? What do we need from God each day? We need his presence, his guidance, and his faithfulness, don't we? If we are to live each day with hope and confidence, we need to be sure that God is with us, God is guiding us, and God will stay with us. But *how can I be sure that God will be with me today, guide me today, and stay with me today?* Let's see how God assured Israel of that in Exodus 40:34–38.[1]

### God Is with Us 40:33–34

"So Moses finished the work" (Ex. 40:33). God had given Moses the tabernacle plans from Exodus 25 to 35. God moved the people to fund the construction in Exodus 36. Then God helped Moses and the craftsmen throughout the building process from Exodus 37–40. In Exodus 40:33, we read these simple words: *So Moses finished the work.*

The very next verse says, "Then the cloud covered the tent of meeting, and the glory of the LORD filled the tabernacle" (40:34). Now that's an opening ceremony! As soon as Moses hung the last exterior curtain, God's glory exploded to cover and fill the whole building. What an awesome moment that must have been. God's

1 Chapters 37–40 largely cover the construction of the tabernacle and its furniture, the meaning of which we studied in the earlier chapters where God gave the plans to Moses.

message to Israel was unmistakable: "I am here. I am with you." Remember, he was not with them directly, but in and through the tabernacle, the place of sacrificial death and blood-bought forgiveness.

***God forgives us to live with us.***

*"But how do I know where to turn, where to go in life?"*
*We turn to our life guide.*

## God Guides Us 40:36–37

God's presence wasn't static but dynamic. "Throughout all their journeys, whenever the cloud was taken up from over the tabernacle, the people of Israel would set out. But if the cloud was not taken up, then they did not set out till the day that it was taken up" (40:36–37). Every day, the first thing Israel did was look to the tabernacle to see if God's glory was in it or above it. If it was still in it, they stayed put. If it was above it, God was moving and therefore so were they.

***If you want God's guidance through the day,***
***get with God first thing in the morning.***

*"Will he be there every day?"*
*Every single day.*

## God Stays with Us 40:38

"For the cloud of the LORD was on the tabernacle by day, and fire was in it by night, in the sight of all the house of Israel throughout all their journeys" (40:38). These are the last words of Exodus. Do you remember the first words? Chapter 1 began with Israel in pagan Egypt enslaved, oppressed, groaning, and crying. The book ends with Israel free from Egypt and filled with God. As we've discovered, they were a far-from-perfect people. And yet God stayed with them throughout their journey. He never left them or forsook them. Every morning they saw his glory cloud. Every night before going to bed they could see his glory fire. What a comfort!

*When God lives with us,*
*he never leaves us.*

## Changing Our Story with God's Story

We don't have a tabernacle, so how does God live with us today? "And the Word became flesh and dwelt (lit., *tabernacled*) among us, and we have seen his glory, glory as of the only Son from the Father, full of grace and truth" (John 1:14). Through faith in Jesus, God's glory is with us, guides us, and stays with us.

**Summary:** How can I be sure that God will be with me today, guide me today, and stay with me today? *Have daily confidence in the God who is with us, guides us, and stays with us through Jesus.*

**Question:** How has Exodus changed your view of God's redemption and of your relationship with God?

**Prayer:** My Redeemer, thank you for bringing me into relationship with you through Jesus Christ. Help me to live a life worthy of a redeemed slave and a royal child.

## TheStoryChanger.life

To keep changing your story with God's Story, visit www.thestory changer.life for the latest news about more StoryChanger devotionals, to sign up for the StoryChanger newsletter, and to subscribe to *The StoryChanger* podcast.